Buddhist-Christian Dialogue
in an Age of Science

Buddhist-Christian Dialogue in an Age of Science

Paul O. Ingram

ROWMAN & LITTLEFIELD PUBLISHERS, INC.
Lanham • Boulder • New York • Toronto • Plymouth, UK

ROWMAN & LITTLEFIELD PUBLISHERS, INC.

Published in the United States of America
by Rowman & Littlefield Publishers, Inc.
A wholly owned subsidiary of The Rowman & Littlefield Publishing Group, Inc.
4501 Forbes Boulevard, Suite 200, Lanham, Maryland 20706
www.rowmanlittlefield.com

Estover Road
Plymouth PL6 7PY
United Kingdom

British Library Cataloguing in Publication Information Available

Library of Congress Cataloging-in-Publication Data
Ingram, Paul O., 1939–
  Buddhist-Christian dialogue in an age of science / Paul O. Ingram.
    p. cm.
  ISBN-13: 978-0-7425-6214-1 (cloth : alk. paper)
  ISBN-10: 0-7425-6214-X (cloth : alk. paper)
  ISBN-13: 978-0-7425-6215-8 (pbk. : alk. paper)
  ISBN-10: 0-7425-6215-8 (pbk. : alk. paper)
  1. Religion and science. 2. Christianity and other religions—Buddhism. 3. Buddhism—
Relations—Christianity. I. Title.
  BL240.3.I54 2008
  261.2'43—dc22   2007019517

Printed in the United States of America

∞™ The paper used in this publication meets the minimum requirements of
American National Standard for Information Sciences—Permanence of Paper
for Printed Library Materials, ANSI/NISO Z39.48-1992.

~

Contents

~

Preface

It might seem a bit odd that someone with my academic training should write a book about Buddhist-Christian dialogue with the natural sciences. I began my academic career as a historian of religions who specialized in Japanese Buddhism. But during my years of undergraduate teaching, I also taught courses in South Asian and East Asian religious traditions, as well as a course on Islam. History of religions is a descriptive discipline that tends to shy away from the normative sorts of questions that concern philosophers and theologians. So, I early on focused on helping my students *understand* the religious history, thought, and practices of traditions other than those of the majority of my students. My focus as historian of religions is on *what* religious human beings have believed and practiced, not whether they *should* believe or practice what they do. The normative questions I have left to the theologians and philosophers.

But after about five years of teaching experience, I discovered just how artificial the distinction between "descriptive" and "normative" questions is. No matter how hard I tried to avoid normative questions, the "ought to believe and do" questions, and focused on what religious people believe and do, the more my students wouldn't let me get away with it. The very act of understanding the pluralism of religious experience and practices raises normative questions of meaning and truth, and I soon discovered that my students' normative questions were similar to my own. So, I began focusing my pedagogical efforts on helping students develop their own sense of religious truth contextualized by what I could descriptively teach them about the world's religious traditions.

Thus, my training in history of religions became the foundation for my own personal theological and philosophical journey. Descriptive questions and normative questions are interdependent, so in my later work I often wore two methodological hats simultaneously, that of historian of religion and that of Lutheran Christian interested in dialogue between the world's religions. This became the focus of my writing, although I never stopped doing research and writing in the field of Japanese Buddhism. This, in turn, led me in 1980 to participate in contemporary Buddhist-Christian dialogue, mostly within the context of the Society for Buddhist-Christian Studies, an association of Buddhist and Christian scholars, as well as other persons interested in this particular dialogue.

Finally, about ten years ago, I became interested in science-religion dialogue, which I first experienced through my association with the Center for Theology and the Natural Sciences (CTNS) in Berkeley, California, and the Center for Process Studies in Claremont, California, which has also continued to nurture my interest in process theology and philosophy. The science-religion dialogue that occurs at CTNS is mostly science-Christian dialogue, although occasionally Jewish and Muslim dialogue with the sciences is also published in the CTNS journal, *Theology and Science*. The same is true for other science-religions dialogues occurring throughout North America and Western Europe. This fact has been recognized by the leaders of CTNS, most notably its founder, Robert John Russell, and scholars like Ian Barbour, John B. Cobb Jr., and John F. Haught. Inspired by the work of these writers, I began to investigate the possibilities of incorporating the natural sciences into current Buddhist-Christian dialogue as a third partner: *Buddhist-Christian Dialogue with the Natural Sciences*.

Six preliminary observations serve as presuppositions for the interpretative framework of this study. First, much of the current discussion on the relation between the natural sciences and religion rests on a confusion between ideology and theory. Charles Darwin's understanding of evolution through natural selection was for him a theory that described such biological processes as the origin of species and the biological interdependence of all living organisms. But even in his own time, ardent supporters of Darwin, like Thomas Huxley, transformed his evolutionary theory into a reductionist discourse that assumed a materialist metaphysics according to which whole disciplines of thought—history, economics, political theory, religion, the humanities in general—were interpreted through the lenses of natural selection and survival of the fittest. Of course, economics, politics, and religion are connected to biological processes since human beings conduct their lives and plan for the future through these areas of thought. But Darwin, unlike many of his defenders, never reduced economics, politics, and religion to biological processes. He, unlike Huxley, was not a reductionist ideologue, even though he was, in his later life, a materialist in his understanding of natural history. In this regard, Darwin was no different from any other nineteenth-century naturalist.

Second, contemporary scientific materialists of the likes of Richard Dawkins, Jacques Monod, E. O. Wilson, or Steven Weinberg are current disciples of Huxley's materialist reductionism. They have transformed their practice of science into an ideology that has an answer for every question about the structure of reality—even before anyone asks a question. Just how do organic molecules become living organisms? Through evolutionary natural selection. Why do human beings have greater intelligence than other life-forms on planet Earth, far more intelligence than is required for survival and procreation? Because of evolutionary natural selection. Evolution is portrayed as the cause of everything, a sort of modern version of Aristotle's unmoved mover.

So, while Jewish, Christian, and Muslim theists who take science seriously usually attribute the orderliness of the physical processes of nature to God, just as Buddhists who take the natural sciences seriously usually attribute this same orderliness to karma, scientific materialists attribute everything to the chance interactions of matter. In truth, the natural sciences have made amazing advances since Galileo looked through his telescope at the moons of Jupiter and the mountains on the moon. And in defensive reaction, more conservative religious believers, illustrated by Christian fundamentalism and the intelligent design movement, have worked hard to find "gaps" in scientific explanations of nature in order to promote divine explanations for scientific mysteries.

Yet, surely, "God of the gaps explanations" of natural processes are as incoherent as materialist explanations because both are reductionist explanations, but in their own, distinctive ways. As a God of the gaps engenders incoherent theology and bad science, the reductionisms of scientific materialism engender equally bad science. This is so because contemporary scientific materialists have devised their own replacement for the God of the gaps of Christian fundamentalism: "materialism of the gaps" to patch up holes in the scientific understanding of such areas as the origins of life and consciousness in the universe. Everything, we nonmaterialists are assured, will eventually be explained in terms of the functions and emergent properties of physical processes.

Third, this raises real questions that materialists have as yet not bothered to confront. Why should anyone make the leap of faith that the materialist assertion that everything human beings experience conforms to human notions of "physical"? Even if it does, to which theory of matter does reality—the way things really are—conform? According to Newtonian physics, a material object is a fraction of space endowed with physical properties, such as impenetrability and mass. But these concepts are replaced by quantum physics, which undermines the Newtonian conception of matter as a collection of inherently passive and spatially defined particulate bodies. In fact, the more physicists and biologists learn about the fundamental constituents of nature, the clearer it is becoming that matter is not composed of "matter" but of oscillations of immaterial entities in empty space. In other words, scientific materialists fill in the gaps in their knowledge with abstractions having no relation to actual physical realities, what Alfred North Whitehead called "the fallacy of misplaced concreteness."

But there is something else. One hypothesis in quantum physics, championed by John Archibald Wheeler, is that without reference to an observer, the universe as a whole does not change in time.[1] If this turns out to be the case, the materialist interpretation of evolution through natural selection over time will require extensive revision. Or, as psychobiologists insist that the mind be explained in terms of biology, biophysicists insist that living organisms be explained in terms of physics, while mathematical physicists insist that the physical universe be explained in terms of mathematics. But mathematics seems inseparable from the human mind, and so reductionism seems to have come full circle.

Fourth, in spite of the great successes of methodological reductionism in contemporary scientific methods, reductionism has severe limitations. Mathematical theories alone do not define, predict, or explain the emergence of the physical universe. Physical theories alone do not define, predict, or explain the emergence of life in the universe. Biological theories alone do not define, predict, or explain the emergence of consciousness in living organisms. The ideology of scientific materialism is simply based on the closure principle—in similarity to the principle of the conservation of energy in physics—which states that there are no nonphysical influences or explanations operative in the physical universe. Yet, the actual nature of energy and matter as it exists in the universe remains a mystery, and there is no scientific consensus about what "makes" something "physical." Accordingly, belief in scientific materialism requires faith in postulates that are every bit as abstract as those commonly found in religion, particularly Christian theology and Buddhist philosophy.

Fifth, science has always closely interacted with the prevailing religious traditions of its host cultures. Current materialist interpretations of evolution are, for example, intertwined with eighteenth-century Enlightenment metaphysics, which portrayed the universe as causally closed to all nonphysical influences. But the natural sciences may also be understood within the context of twenty-first-century notions of a "participatory universe" revealed through intersubjective experience. It is here that dialogue between the sciences and the world's religious traditions, in this book illustrated by Buddhist-Christian conceptual dialogue with the natural sciences as a third partner, might serve to transform creatively both the natural sciences and Buddhist and Christian thought and practice.

If, finally, we do inhabit a "participatory universe," a primary task for thinking religious people in an age of science will be to rethink the meaning of scripture, doctrine, and practice in light of scientific accounts of physical processes. This process will require dialogical engagement with all the disciplines of the physical sciences. In particular, it is vital for Buddhists and Christians to understand the radical changes now occurring in our current understanding of physical reality and the effect these changes can positively and negatively have on the specifics of Buddhist and Christian self-understanding and practice. To the degree that Buddhists and Christians choose not to engage the sciences in dialogue, Buddhism and Christianity will become irrelevant to the lives of Buddhist and Christian persons who must struggle for meaning in a scientific age. Thus, the overriding thesis of *Buddhist-Christian Dialogue in an Age of Science*—incorporating the natural sciences as a third partner in contemporary Buddhist-Christian dialogue—will creatively transform Buddhism, Christianity, *and* the natural sciences.

Each of the following chapters aims to defend this thesis with a general summary of how Buddhists and Christians have engaged scientific cosmology, evolutionary theory, and the neurosciences. Of course, there are other scientific disciplines that other writers could choose to demonstrate this thesis, but I have chosen the scientific disciplines with which I am most familiar. The intention of these chapters is to describe the challenges specific sciences have posed to Buddhism and Christianity, as well as areas where Christians and Buddhists have experienced consonance with these sciences. The final chapter is more speculative in nature because it is concerned with how Buddhist-Christian dialogue with the natural sciences might contribute to the creative transformation of the sciences.

Writers need critical readers, especially in the preliminary stages of the writing process before a project assumes its published form. Critical readers are the best friends an author can have, and I wish to express my gratitude to

Brian Romer, an acquisitions editor with Rowman & Littlefield. Two years ago, Brian asked me to consider writing a book on Buddhist-Christian dialogue with the natural sciences. His generous encouragement and support of this project is deeply appreciated. Elaine McGarraugh supervised the editing of this project. Her work was crucial in creating a text more readable than the original manuscript, and I am deeply grateful. While any of the weaknesses of *Buddhist-Christian Dialogue in an Age of Science* are entirely my responsibility, I suspect that the strengths this book might have are mostly due to the criticism of these two professionals.

Finally, I want to dedicate this book to my wife, Regina Inslee Ingram, who has been my best critic and support for forty-three years.

Note

1. John Archibald Wheeler, *At Home in the Universe* (New York: AIP Press, 1996), 295–311.

CHAPTER ONE

~

A Common Cosmology

Charles H. Townes, 1964 Nobel Prize Laureate in physics and 2005 Templeton Prize Laureate, characterizes the close relation between science and religion as a convergence emerging from the similarities they share in common
in spite of differences.[1] Both science and religion seek to explain (1) how the
universe works and (2) how the meaning of the universe works. While science and religion do not draw identical conclusions about the universe, the
parallels between them are certainly as striking as the differences. As science
seeks to understand what the physical universe is like and how it works, including human beings, so religion aims at understanding the meaning and
purpose of the universe, including the meaning of human life. According to
Townes, science and religion are best understood as complementary human
ways of understanding the structure of existence because if it is true that the
universe does have purpose and meaning, whatever meaning there is must be
reflected in the physical structures of the universe that engage the natural
sciences along with the search for meaning that engages religious persons.
Science and religion are not rivals.

Townes is one of a rapidly growing number of scientists and religious
thinkers who argue that reductionist programs in the sciences and metaphysics have suffered a major, and probably fatal, setback. It is crucial that
scientists and religious persons understand how this setback has occurred.
First, physics has encountered empirical evidence that makes the search for
a single, explanatory "theory of everything" from which all the universe's
physical phenomena can be derived an epistemological dead end; relativity

theory introduced the speed of light as the absolute limit for velocity, which means there is a limit for communication and causation in the universe; Heisenberg's uncertainty principle placed mathematical limits on knowing both the location and the velocity of a subatomic particle; the "Copenhagen interpretation" of quantum theory concludes that quantum mechanical indeterminacy is not simply a temporary gap in human knowledge, but reflects the inherent indeterminacy of the universe itself; chaos theory shows that future states of complex systems (like weather systems) are so sensitive to their initial conditions that no one can ever predict the evolution of the system as a whole, which is a staggering limitation in light of the number of natural systems that exhibit chaotic behaviors; and Kurt Gödel mathematically proved that even mathematics can never be complete.

Of course, *epistemological reductionism*, the attempt to understand natural processes in terms of their constituent parts and the laws that determine their relationships, still characterizes the daily practice of working scientists and will continue to do so in the future. But *metaphysical reductionism* has started to lose its hold on the natural sciences, which opens up new avenues for exploring the relationships between the natural sciences and philosophy and religion. Of course, metaphysical reductionism has not completely disappeared. Scientific materialists like Richard Dawkins, Steven Weinberg, and E. O. Wilson still gain publicity for their antireligion views based on their assumption that the only knowledge persons can achieve about any subject is what a reductionist scientific method can validate experimentally. But a vastly larger number of scientists and philosophers of science are now working with postreductionist paradigms.

It is reasonable, therefore, to conclude that studying either science or religion might tell us something about the other, as well as something about structures of the universe. Furthermore, understanding either science or religion requires the use of logic, evidence (rational analysis of experience in religion, experimentation in the sciences), carefully chosen assumptions, intuition, and faith. It is at the point of faith that the convergence between science and religion starts, which in turn constitutes the foundation for dialogue between the sciences and religion in general, as well as the thesis of this book: bringing the natural sciences into contemporary Buddhist-Christian dialogue as a third partner will engender the mutual creative transformation of Buddhism, Christianity, and the natural sciences.

It is abundantly clear that faith is as operationally important for scientists as it for religious persons. Of course, much depends on the meaning of the word "faith." According to popular English usage, "faith" is the assertion of an opinion without sufficient evidence to call one's opinion "knowledge," as illustrated by the notion that religious ideas or Christian doctrines like the Incarnation or the Resurrection of Christ must be accepted "on faith," apart from rational argument for or against these doctrines. But this is to misunderstand the meaning of faith as taught in all the world religions.[2] Faith is never the irrational act of willing to believe something is true or false in spite of evidence to support such belief, as in the notion that something must be "accepted on faith." In a religious or a scientific context, faith is an act of trust, a way of "betting one's life," that involves the whole person, that is, the intellect, the emotions, and the body, and it is thereby the foundation for knowing anything at all, as in St. Anselm's formulation, "faith seeking understanding." Beliefs may be elegant, informed, uninformed, stupid, superstitious, true, or false. Beliefs may even express faith. But beliefs, as such, can neither *be* faith nor *engender* faith. So, whether scientist or religious practitioner, one *finds* oneself *in* a state of faith; one does not *believe* oneself *into* a state of faith. Whether in a scientific or a religious context, betting one's life on an "opinion" is a highly irrational act and never conducive to attaining knowledge. It is also an act of "unfaith." However, once finding oneself in a state of faith, one is able to draw reasonable conclusions and beliefs that sometimes constitute real knowledge.

Yet, it is certainly not widely understood that the natural sciences involve assumptions based on faith. Scientists trust that a rational order underlies the structure of the physical processes of the universe, but they can't "prove" it through scientific methods. Without this trust, science cannot proceed. Accordingly, nothing in the natural sciences is absolutely proven. It was the mathematician Gödel who showed logically that to prove something, there must be an overall set of assumptions, but we can never prove that these assumptions are even self-consistent. We must make the best assumptions based on reasoning about experience we can and have faith, that is, trust, that this will engender knowledge about the structures of natural processes. The result is powerful knowledge of the physical universe that is always incomplete, always capable of revision, because it is never completely certain. As in religion, it is "faith seeking understanding" that engenders imperfect knowledge always in need of revision.

The role of faith in scientific method is evident because there are as many mysteries in science as there are in religion. For example, physicists know only about 5 percent of the matter and energy comprising the universe. What is the nature of the remaining 95 percent, now vaguely referred to as "dark matter" and "dark energy," matter and energy being two sides of the same physical reality, according to Albert Einstein's theory of special relativity? It is clearly detectible in the universe's expansion, but at this date, *what* dark matter or energy *is* remains a mystery. Scientists also assume the laws of physics have been the same everywhere in the universe from that point of time after the Big Bang called Plank time until the present.[3] Scientists trust this to be true, with good reason, but do not know if these laws could change or are, in fact, the same everywhere in the universe, or in multiple universes—if multiple universes exist.

Given the convergence between science and religion that Townes describes, the current science-religion dialogue should be of mutual benefit to scientists, Buddhists, and Christians. The most expedient means of beginning the argument in support of this conclusion is to focus on the origin story of the universe, coupled with current scientific speculation about the universe's probable end. It must be understood, however, that this cosmological picture is undergoing continual modification as new evidence is discovered. Not all cosmologists are in agreement with standard Big Bang cosmology, so the version I describe here is a "majority report" based on this standard model. While in many ways constituting a challenge to all traditional religious beliefs and practices, Big Bang cosmology also provides a common narrative that is capable of inclusion in the wisdom of all religious traditions in their own distinctive ways. It is also the scientific starting point for any religious tradition's dialogue with the natural sciences.

The Common Cosmological Narrative

According to the standard model, some 13.5 billion years ago, the contents of the universe were together in an initial singularity, meaning a region of infinite curvature and energy density at which the known laws of physics break down ($t = 0$).[4] There was a "big bang." The history of the cosmos began approximately three minutes after this event, when protons and neutrons were combining to form nuclei. Five hundred thousand years later, atoms were coming into existence. One billion years from $t = 0$, galaxies and stars were being formed, followed by planets at ten billion years. After another two billion years, microscopic forms of life were beginning to appear on our planet.

A universe without life is a different universe with life, which means that part of this origin narrative must include the origin of life, both on this planet and most probably elsewhere in the universe. The fact of evolution has been scientifically established with the kind of certainty attributable to such concepts as the roundness of the Earth, the heliocentric motions of the planets, and the molecular composition of matter. Evolution is descent with modification over time. All living organisms today share common descent with modification from microbial life of the simplest type—called *prokary-*

otes, which are cells whose nuclear material is not bounded by a nuclear membrane—which existed about three billion years ago. The process driving evolution is natural selection, which is a process of change and diversification in living forms over time that seems rooted in the genetic structure of all living organisms. Apparently, evolution does not reverse itself but is unidirectional toward the future, much like what cosmologists call the "arrow of time," which can never, as far as anyone knows, reverse itself.

What this cosmological narrative demonstrates is that all things and events that ever have been, now are, or ever will be are interrelated and interdependent from the very beginning. We are relatives of the stars, the oceans, the Earth, and all creatures that have lived, now live, or will live. The entire universe is interrelated and organic in structure, a dynamic reality, constantly moving and becoming, always in process. This implies that the universe is radically open ended, creative of ever new novelty, things and events never before imagined, yet always coming to be, in interdependence with all that went on before—ideas that should bring a smile of recognition to all Buddhists as well as Christian process theologians.

While scientific cosmology cannot simply replace the basic content of religious creation myths, current scientific cosmology can clarify and transform religious creation myths. As any lived myth does, scientific cosmology gives expression to religious experiences and convictions that are already present in most religious communities; it is a common origin story that is available to be remythologized by most religious traditions in terms of their own specific history and practices. Accordingly, scientific cosmology is a place of meeting for the world's religions. Furthermore, this common story of the universe, with its revelation of universal interdependence and interrelationship, provides us with a means for breaking the roadblocks that many postmodern thinkers put up before any universal ethical venture or truth claim. To the postmodern insistence—itself a universal truth claim that is, when pushed to its logical conclusion, incoherent with its own assumptions—that every theological and religious claim based on universal criteria is nothing but a social construction of the politically powerful, valid only for its own backyard, we can hold up a common origin story of the universe that tells us that (and how) we are interrelated and interdependent.

In asserting that scientific cosmology provides us with a "metadiscourse" of the universe by which it is possible to link individual discourses, such as theology, ethics, or politics, or the teachings and practices of different religious traditions, I am not claiming that scientific conclusions provide universal criteria for judging all truth claims, or that truth claims can be neatly and easily articulated by means of interreligious dialogue with the natural sciences. Furthermore, it is wise not to dismiss uncritically the specter of postmodernism's most important warning. As it is always dangerous to identify what is common in human experience in general, it is equally dangerous to identify what is common in humanity's religious experience in particular. Yet, we are not condemned to the debilitating relativism that postmodernists tell us is ingredient in the personal or communal construction of perspectives from which we are free to make any selection we wish as we shop through the history of ideas. As the Buddhist deconstructionist Nagarjuna taught in India in the second century BC, there is always a middle way between certainty and relativism, which I think corresponds to critical realism's advice that we adhere to rational beliefs held with conviction but open to the likelihood of correction.

But there is more to this narrative. In 1988, two groups of astrophysicists, one led by Brian Schmidt and the other by Saul Perlmutter, using similar techniques, were looking for a specific kind of explosion called a "type 1a supernova," which occurs when an aging star destroys itself in a gigantic thermonuclear blast. Type 1a supernovas are so bright that their light can be seen all the way across the universe and is uniform enough to have its distance from Earth calculated with a great degree of accuracy. This is important because, as Edwin Hubbell discovered, the whole universe is expanding in all directions at any time, and more distant galaxies are receding from Earth faster than nearby galaxies. So, Schmidt's and Perlmutter's teams measured the distance to these supernovas (deduced from their brightness) and their speed of recession (deduced by the reddening of their light known as the Doppler shift).

When this information was finally gathered and analyzed, both teams knew something very quirky was going on. In the 1980s, astrophysicists thought the universe's expansion would eventually slow down, either gradually or rapidly, depending on the amount of matter contained in the universe, an effect that was expected to show up as distant supernovas looking brighter than one would expect when compared to closer supernovas. In fact, these distant supernovas were dimmer, which meant that the universe's expansion was speeding up, which in turn suggested that some sort of powerful "dark energy," now called antigravity, is forcing the galaxies to fly apart against the gravity drawing them together. This means there is now more antigravity pushing the galaxies apart at an accelerating rate than there is gravity pulling the galaxies together—which means the universe will continue to expand forever unless forces now unknown to science are at work.

So, given what cosmologists conclude about the universe's origins according to Big Bang theory and the fact that the universe will most probably infinitely expand, a picture of the universe's final end seems to be emerging in the scientific community. The hundred billion or so galaxies that can now be observed through the Hubbell telescope and telescopes on Earth will zip out of range. Tens of billions of years from now, the Milky Way will be the only galaxy detectable from Earth, although it's unlikely anything will be alive on our planet by then. Other nearby galaxies, including the Large Magellanic Cloud and the Andromeda Galaxy, will have drifted into and merged with the Milky Way. The sun will have shrunken to a white dwarf, giving little light and less heat to whatever is left on Earth, and entered into a long, lingering death that could last a hundred trillion years—or a thousand times longer than the universe has existed to the present date. The same will happen to most other stars, although a few will end as blazing supernovas. All that will be left will be black holes, the burnt out residue of stars, and whatever remains of dead planets. Finally, by the time the universe is one trillion trillion trillion trillion trillion trillion years old, these black holes themselves will disintegrate into stray particles, which will bind loosely enough to form individual "atoms" the size of today's universe. Eventually, even these will decay, leaving a featureless, infinitely large void. And that will be that—if this account of the universe's end is accurate or unless whatever inconceivable event that launched the original Big Bang should recur.

Astronomers and physicists are a very cautious lot, and they insist that the mind-bending discoveries about dark matter, dark energy, and the apparent flatness of space-time must be confirmed before they can be finally accepted. There could be more surprises to come: the idea of a cosmological constant— a notion Einstein repudiated as his biggest mistake—is now the leading candidate for understanding dark energy. However, dark energy could be something altogether different, perhaps a force that could even reverse directions at some future point in space-time and reinforce, rather than oppose, gravity. If, however, these discoveries do hold up, some of the most important questions in cosmology—the universe's age, what it's made of, and how it will end—will be answered only seventy years after they were first posed. And well before the end of cosmic history—further in the future than human minds can grasp—humanity, and perhaps even biology, will have vanished. Yet, it is conceivable that consciousness of some sort may survive, perhaps in the form of a disembodied digital intelligence.[5] If so, this intelligence will notice that the universe, once ablaze with light from uncountable stars, has become a vast, cold, dark, lonely void.

If this is really all there is, the universe indeed seems pointless and empty of value, and the metaphysical conclusions Steven Weinberg draws from Big Bang cosmology, Richard Dawkins's interpretation of evolutionary history, and E. O. Wilson's theories of social biology and genetic determinism appear as accurate descriptions of reality—the way things really are, as opposed to the way religious persons would like things to be. The challenges these metaphysical interpretations of the cosmological narrative pose for all religious traditions are crystal clear. Christian, Jewish, and Islamic doctrines and practices, every one of them, are illusions having no basis in physical fact. Theravada and Mahayana Buddhist doctrines and practices, Hindu tradition, and Confucian and Taoist traditions, as well as the primal traditions of Native Americans and other tribal cultures, are likewise illusory. None of humanity's religious ways can have any ontological correspondence to reality. This means that all Christian theologies of religion—exclusivist, inclusivist, or pluralistic—are meaningless—which means that the practice of interreligious dialogue as a form of theological interaction with the natural sciences is a reflection on ideas without ontological correspondence to anything that can actually exist. In short, the practice of interreligious dialogue with the natural sciences is based on an illusion and is a waste of energy.

Yet, as John Polkinghorne reminds us, scientific inquiry is very narrow and limited—bits and pieces of physical processes of nature that can be analyzed through repeatable experimental procedures described mathematically.[6] The fact is that the brilliant intellectual power and success of the natural sciences in revealing the physical processes of the universe and the technological applications of scientific knowledge come at the price of ignoring most of what human beings experience. For example, while the methodological reductionisms of physics can easily explain why we hear sounds because of the vibration of air molecules striking our eardrums, physics cannot explain my or anyone else's love of jazz or classical music or the poetry of William Butler Yeats or of T. S. Elliot, or why people prefer other styles of music or other poets. While biology can accurately explain the evolutionary history of the human eye, it cannot explain why the alternating light show on Puget Sound on an autumn day, when the sun breaks through slate gray rain clouds and paints the water and trees in acrylic fall colors, always stuns me to silence. From the wider parameters of human experience, the materialist reductionisms of Weinberg, Wilson, and Dawkins seem more like incoherent metaphysics than scientific description.

It is also a fact that none of the religious traditions of humanity assume that scientific theories and descriptions of physical reality describe "all there is." As John Hick never tires of pointing out, all religious human beings share a common "religious intention" not to delude themselves about the way things really are in this universe,[7] which is not to say that religious persons do not often delude themselves. Karl Marx was partly right. Religious faith and practice can be and often is an opiate, an anesthesia that deadens one's intellect and emotions, a prophylactic to shield oneself from contamination from the disagreeable realities of existence or from religious traditions, cultures, and people one regards as "other." But Marx was also partly wrong. Historically, the most creative human advances are in what the Chinese called *wen*, or the "arts" that civilize human beings. It is the arts, culture in its widest meanings, that place persons in contact with reality and with what is distinctive about being human. The arts of all cultures, including the natural sciences, are historically grounded in the religious traditions of those cultures. For example, the brilliance of Chinese culture during the T'ang and Sung dynasties was rooted in Confucian and Buddhist sources; the European Renaissance owes its beginnings to the Islamic culture of the House of Wisdom in twelfth-century Damascus and later in Andalusian Spain; and the art, music, and political and economic philosophies of Europe, as well as the natural sciences, have their theological and philosophical foundations in Jewish, Christian, and Islamic thought.

Surely, the experiences and teachings of the Buddha, Mohammed's experience as a messenger called to recite God's words to his people, the historical Jesus's experience of the Kingdom of God and God's call to enter this kingdom in obedience to the demands of radical love, Hindu experience of Brahman as one's deepest self, Confucius's sensitivity to the moral foundations of the natural order, or the experiences of sacred power in the forces of nature in Native American experience are not collective illusions. I cannot prove it, but I find it difficult to believe that collective illusions can hang around in human history for as long as Buddhism, Christianity, Islam, Hinduism, Confucianism, and Native American cultures have endured. Human beings are often collectively and individually delusional but probably not for as long as the world's religious traditions have existed.

Yet, if it is confirmed that the universe's expansion continues forever, the universe in fact seems condemned to futility, and human existence is a transient episode in its history. Such a bleak prognosis of the universe's destiny certainly puts in question the evolutionary optimism of such writers as Pierre Teilhard de Chardin, who posits a final fulfillment of existence solely within the confines of the unfolding of physical processes as a final "Omega point."[8] Such notions seem particularly irrelevant given what physicists are now understanding about the universe's origins and destiny. Furthermore, it is clear that current cosmological speculation about the origins and end of the universe constitutes an important challenge to the relevance of humanity's religious traditions.

A Typology of Dialogue

Because Buddhists and Christians engage in dialogue for different reasons, it is useful to describe three major forms of dialogue that have evolved in contemporary Buddhist-Christian encounters over the past twenty years: "conceptual dialogue," "socially engaged dialogue," and "interior dialogue." The boundaries separating these three forms of dialogue are not always clear. Most Christian theologians stress "conceptual dialogue" in their encounter with Buddhism, but a growing number emphasize "socially engaged dialogue," while Christians interested in such spiritual disciplines as contemplative prayer and meditation focus on "interior dialogue."

Conceptual Dialogue

The focus of conceptual dialogue is doctrinal, theological, and philosophical. It concerns a religious tradition's self-understanding and worldview. In conceptual dialogue, Buddhists and Christians compare theological and philosophical formulations on such questions as ultimate reality, human nature, suffering and evil, the role of Jesus in Christian faith and the role of the Buddha in Buddhist practice, and what Christians and Buddhists can conceptually learn from one another.

Few theologians have conceptually engaged Buddhism more systematically and incorporated Buddhist thought into their theologies more intentionally than process theologian John B. Cobb Jr. In fact, Cobb is one of the first major theologians to appropriate the scholarship of history of religions, particularly in regard to Buddhism, as an object of his theological reflection. His conversation with Buddhism is grounded in the notion that interreligious dialogue is a conceptual process of passing "beyond dialogue."[9] Passing beyond dialogue does not mean the practice of dialogue needs to stop, since continued growth in Christian faith is the purpose of Christian dialogue with other religious traditions. Cobb assumes the same process also occurs for Buddhists, who, faithful to Buddhist tradition, go beyond dialogue with Christian theological reflection. Accordingly, "passing beyond dialogue" names the process of continual theological engagement *in* dialogue as a contributive element *to* one's tradition.

For Cobb, dialogue is itself a theological practice that involves two interdependent movements: (1) in dialogue with Buddhists, Christians should intentionally leave the conventional boundaries of Christian tradition and enter into Buddhist thought and experience; (2) this is followed by a return to the home of Christian faith enriched, renewed, and "creatively transformed," which is part of what Cobb means by "passing beyond dialogue." The goal of interreligious dialogue for Christians is "creative transformation," defined as a process of critically appropriating whatever one has learned from dialogue into one's own faith and practice, whereby one's faith is challenged, enriched, and renewed. For Christians, the image of creative transformation is Christ, who explicitly provides a focal point of unity within which the many centers of meaning that characterize the present age of religious pluralism, as well as the natural sciences, are harmonized. Since Cobb thinks that no truth can be foreign to the truth Christians experience engendered by faith in Christ, Christians can and should be open to the "structures of existence" of the other "religious ways" of humanity.[10] However, appropriating Buddhist doctrines into one's theological reflection does not entail imposing Christian meanings onto Buddhism or the sciences. Conceptual dialogue that leads to the creative transformation of Christian faith should falsify neither Christian nor Buddhist experience nor the natural sciences.

Socially Engaged Dialogue

Although Buddhists have emphasized socially engaged dialogue with Christians more than conceptual dialogue, Christian conceptual dialogue with Buddhists has also generated interest in the relevance of Buddhist thought and practice to issues of social, environmental, economic, and gender justice. Since these issues are systemic, global, interconnected, and interdependent, they are not religion or culture specific. Participants in all religious traditions have experienced these forms of oppression. Accordingly, Christians and Buddhists have apprehended common experiences and resources for working together to liberate human beings and nature from global forces of systemic oppression.

The term *social engagement* was first coined in 1963 by the Vietnamese Zen Buddhist monk Thich Nhat Hahn as a description of the Buddhist antiwar movement in Vietnam and is now the most common term describing Buddhist social activism.[11] Some Christian liberation theologians have also appropriated this term in their theological reflection. At the heart of Buddhist traditions of social engagement are the doctrines of interdependence and nonviolence. Interdependence (*pratītya-samutpāda*, or "dependent coarising") is the doctrine that all things and events at every moment of space-time are constituted by their interrelationships with all other things and events, so that nothing exists in separation from other things and events. All things and events are mutually cocreated by this web of interrelationships. Since these relationships are always in a state of change and process, all things and events are in a constant state of change and becoming. Impermanence is therefore ingredient in the structure of existence itself. Because no thing or event is ever separate from any other thing and event, all things and events become in a mutual web of impermanent interrelationships. Part of the meaning of "awakening" (*nirvāṇa*) is experiential awareness of dependent coarising, which in turn engenders "compassion" (*karunā*) for all sentient beings. Compassion is awareness that in a mutually interdependent universe, the suffering of others is the suffering of all, which in turn energizes action to relieve sentient beings from suffering. Thus, compassion engenders the practice of nonviolence as the ethical core of Buddhist social activism.

Socially engaged Buddhists are uncompromising in the practice of compassionate nonviolence. This has raised for Christians questions about the relationship between nonviolence and justice. Justice is a central theological category for Christian thought and practice, but notions of justice have not historically played an equivalent role in Buddhism. Christian tradition gives priority to loving engagement with the world as the foundation for establishing justice. So, for Christians, the question is, to what extent does nonviolent compassion toward all sentient beings, even toward aggressors doing harm to whole communities of persons, itself become an occasion for injustice?[12] While justice is not identical with revenge, Christian traditions of social justice demand that those who do harm "not get away with it," which means that the establishment of justice may necessitate the use of violent means. Consequently, while the practice of nonviolent compassion as the ethical norm for Buddhist social engagement has forced Christians to reexamine the relationship between love, justice, and violence in social activism, love as involvement with the world in the struggle for justice has energized Buddhists to examine the relation between the practice of nonviolent compassion and justice. Yet, both Christians and Buddhists seem agreed that working together to resolve justice issues is not only possible but necessary, even as the foundations of Buddhist social engagement and Christian social activist traditions are not identical.

Although a number of theologians are in dialogue with Buddhist traditions of social activism, Paul F. Knitter is perhaps the best-known Christian thinker currently socially engaged in dialogue with Buddhist traditions of social engagement. Knitter posits the existence of a "common context" from which religious persons of different religious traditions, in this case Christianity and Buddhism, can and should enter into dialogue. Drawing on Christian liberation theology, he identifies this common context as "the *preferential option for the poor and nonperson*, meaning the option to work with and for the victims of this world."[13] Consequently, apart from commitment to, and identification with, the poor and the oppressed in the global struggle for justice, conceptual dialogue between Christians and Buddhists remains an elitist enterprise with little relevance to the lives oppressed persons. Fur-thermore, Christians and Buddhists have recognized poverty and oppression as common problems from which human beings need liberation. It is neces-sary, therefore, that Buddhist-Christian dialogue evolve into a shared com-mitment to the liberation of human beings from all forms of oppression. In the common struggle for liberation, Christians and Buddhists share a "com-mon ground" that enables them to hear one another and be mutually cre-atively transformed in the process. Thus, while it is important for Christians and Buddhists to engage conceptually, such dialogue is elitist and irrelevant apart from socially engaged dialogue grounded in the preferential option for the poor and the nonperson.[14]

Interior Dialogue

In the work of most Christians in dialogue with Buddhists, conceptual dia-logue engenders interest in socially engaged dialogue, and both forms of dia-logue have led a few Christians and Buddhists to "interior dialogue." Interior dialogue concentrates on participating in Christian and Buddhist spiritual practices and techniques and reflecting on the resulting experiences. The main concerns of interior dialogue arise directly out of the practice disci-plines of both traditions.

Since spiritual and monastic disciplines continue to energize Catholic ex-perience, while monasticism and disciplines such as contemplative prayer have, since Luther's time, been viewed as forms of "works righteousness" and consequently deemphasized in Protestant tradition, Roman Catholics have been more open to interior dialogue with Buddhists. While a number of Catholic monks, nuns, and members of the laity are interested in this form of encounter with Buddhism, Thomas Merton's encounter with the Dalai Lama and other Tibetan monks, Thai Buddhists monks, and Zen teachings and practices has served as a paradigm for other Catholic thinkers. Merton's specific interest in Buddhism evolved out of his frustration with the state of Catholic monasticism as he had experienced it as a Trappist. Toward the end of his life, he had reached the conclusion that Christian monastic traditions should be reformed by means of dialogue with Buddhist monks and nuns through mutual participation and the sharing of Christian-Buddhist medita-tive techniques and experiences.[15] The purpose of "contemplative dialogue," as he referred to what is now called "interior dialogue," is to discover whether there exist similarities and analogies in Christian and Buddhist experience in spite of the doctrinal differences in Christian and Buddhist thought. He came to the conclusion that while doctrinal differences will always differen-tiate the Christian and Buddhist traditions, doctrinal differences do not invalidate the existential similarities of the experiences engendered by Christian and Buddhist monastic disciplines like contemplative prayer and meditation. For the truth discovered by both Christians and Buddhists is beyond the power of doctrine to delimit and specify in any complete way.[16]

Merton's sudden death on December 10, 1968, while attending a conference on monasticism in Bangkok prevented him from developing his insights into a systematic theology of monastic experience. However, other Catholic theologians have followed Merton's lead, among them Ruben L. F. Habito.

Among Catholic Christians theologically engaged with Buddhism, Habito is unique in that (1) he trained in Zen meditation under Yamada Koun Roshi (1907–1989) and received Yamada Roshi's "seal of approval" (inko) as his "dharma heir" during his years in Japan as a Jesuit, and (2) he is interested in both interior and conceptual dialogue with Buddhism. Accordingly, the focus of Habito's theological encounter with Buddhism is his interior dialogue with Zen Buddhist traditions of practice, which he has incorporated into his particular form of contemplative prayer, along with the reformulation of Christian theological categories in light of this interior dialogue. In this, he is rooted in Roman Catholic traditions of interior dialogue with Buddhism that include Philip Johnston, Thomas Merton, and Thomas Keating.[17]

The central theological question Habito brings to dialogue with Buddhism centers on the question of liberation. Since both Christian and Buddhist practices are methods of experiencing liberation, Habito is interested in the core of Buddhist and Christian identity, symbolized by the Buddha's awakening experience under the Tree of Awakening and by Jesus as the Christ hanging from the cross.

For example, in an essay entitled "The Resurrection of the Dead and Life Everlasting: From a Futuristic to a Realized Christianity," Habito points to two articles in the Apostle's Creed—"I believe in . . . the resurrection of the body and the life everlasting"—as the sources for what he perceives to be the interplay between the "future outlook" and, borrowing a phrase from Zen Buddhist teaching, the "realized outlook" of Christian experience. While both outlooks are interdependent and presuppose faith as trust in the promise of eternal life made manifest in Jesus's life, death, and resurrection (the future aspect), he argues that the resurrection of the body and life everlasting are simultaneously a present reality open to anyone who accepts Christ here and now (the realized aspect). Hence, Christian faith's realized aspect entails the experience of eternal life and resurrection in the here-and-now moment of the experience of faith. Zen's stress on experiencing the liberating insight of awakening in the "here-and-now" moment of experience can help Christians appreciate the "realized aspect" of the Christian experience of liberation more fully. Habito's biblical support for this conclusion is the last judgment scene in Matthew 23:31–46, which proclaims that faith in Jesus as the Christ entails a way of life open to the needs of one's neighbors and that acting accordingly is the gate to a future eternal life experienced in a realized moment of awakened experience here and now.[18]

Chapter Summaries

This book is about Buddhist-Christian conceptual dialogue with the natural sciences, although conceptual dialogue with the natural sciences does have implications for Buddhist and Christian socially engaged and interior dialogue. The goal of Buddhist-Christian conceptual dialogue with the natural sciences is the creative transformation of both traditions. What I mean by this will be spelled out in each chapter of the book.

Chapter 2, "Models of Buddhist-Christian Dialogue with the Natural Sciences," is a comparative analysis of forms of Christian and Buddhist conceptual dialogue with the natural sciences. The model that has become standard for describing the forms of Christian dialogue with the natural sciences is Ian Barbour's typology: (1) conflict, (2) independence, (3) dialogue, and (4) integration. Current Buddhist models of dialogue with the sciences are in some ways similar to Barbour's typology, yet are significantly different because of the distinctive worldview of Buddhism. According to José Cabezón's typology, the main operational Buddhist models are (1) conflict/ambivalence, (2) complementarity, and (3) compatibility/identity. I shall illustrate each of these models with a summary of representative Buddhist and Christian writers currently dialogically engaged with the natural sciences. It should be noted that I have not undertaken a detailed critical analysis of these models; nor have I critiqued them. The intention of this chapter is descriptive and comparative, but I undertake a more critical stance in chapter 6.

Chapter 3, "The Challenge of Contemporary Cosmology," is about Christian and Buddhist responses to contemporary scientific cosmology's metanarrative. Here, the focus will be on Christian theological discussion of the possibility and form of divine action in nature compared with Buddhist nontheistic interpretations of scientific cosmology. The goal of this chapter is also comparative and makes no argument for the superiority of either Christian or Buddhist interpretations of scientific cosmology since science, given the narrowness of its focus on only physical phenomena, can offer no support for or against the specific claims of any religious tradition.

"Christian and Buddhist Responses to Evolutionary Biology" is the topic of chapter 4. This chapter begins with a summary of Darwin's theory of evolution and contemporary neo-Darwinian evolutionary theory, followed by a discussion of Christian theological responses to neo-Darwinism. Here, the discussion focuses on Arthur Peacocke and John F. Haught. Buddhist response to evolutionary theory has centered on ecology and neuroscience, in this chapter illustrated by the Dalai Lama, David Galin, and Matthieu Ricard. As in chapter 3, this chapter is informational and descriptive in character.

All scientific disciplines are interdependent and interrelated, but the collection of disciplines comprising the cognitive sciences, the topic of chapter 5, is often perceived to have special relevance for Buddhists and Christians.[19] The reason seems obvious: the theoretical perspective and research of the cognitive sciences will affect how we think of the human person, the nature of consciousness, the issue of free will, and the nature of religious experience, as well as how we think about ourselves within the larger context of the natural world. The cognitive sciences will directly affect how Christians should think about God and God's relation to the world, since Christians often think of God as a mind or a person, which means relying on the conceptual psychological categories available. While God is not an issue for Buddhists, the cognitive sciences require both Buddhists and Christians to rethink their worldviews and practice traditions. Consequently, the topic of this chapter is how the cognitive sciences might aid Buddhists and Christians in the task of reformulating traditional doctrines and practices in ways reflective of what we can conclude about the physiological processes going on in the brain and central nervous systems, which are the physical foundations for mentality and self-awareness.

Chapter 6, "The Structure of Buddhist-Christian-Science Dialogue," is the concluding chapter of this book. Its intent is more theoretical than that of the previous chapters. Since dialogue is a process in which parties engage, sharing in and benefiting from their interaction, the focus of this chapter is on three questions: (1) What can the sciences contribute to Buddhist and Christian self-understanding and creative transformation? (2) Are there nonoverlapping areas of scientific research and Buddhist-Christian traditions that prohibit Buddhism and Christianity from having any legitimate influences on the practice of science? (3) What are the overlapping areas, and what can the Buddhist and Christian traditions conceptually contribute to the sciences that might engender scientific creative transformation?

Notes

1. Among his other accomplishments in physics, Townes cites his discovery of the principles of the maser, an insight that suddenly occurred to him while sitting on a

park bench in Washington, D.C., in 1951, a revelation "as real as any revelation described in the scriptures." This "insight" lead him directly to the invention of the laser, for which he received the Nobel Prize in Physics in 1964. See "Marriage of Two Minds," *Science and Spirit* (January–February 2006): 36–43.

2. See my discussion of faith in "On the Practice of Faith: A Lutheran's Interior Dialogue with Buddhism," *Buddhist-Christian Studies* 21 (2001): 43–45. Also see two books by Wilfred Cantwell Smith, *Belief in History* (Princeton, NJ: Princeton University Press, 1979), and *Understanding Religious Life* (Belmont, CA: Wadsworth Publishing Company, 1985).

3. This is about 10^{-43} seconds, or the time at which the size of the universe, according to the current Big Bang model, was roughly the Plank length, or more precisely the time it takes for light to travel the Plank length. The Plank length is about 10^{-33} centimeters, the size of the universe at Plank time. Prior to Plank time, the laws of physics seem to break down, or are at least not detectable, which is why cosmologists have not been able to determine the exact nature of the event at $t = 0$.

4. See Jonathan J. Halliwell, "Quantum Cosmology and the Creation of the Universe," in *Cosmology: Historical, Literary, Philosophical, Religious, and Scientific Perspectives* (New York: Garland Publishing, 1993), 477–97.

5. See Frank Tipler, "The Omega Point as *Eschaton*: Answers to Pannenberg's Questions for Scientists," *Zygon* 24, no 2 (June 1989): 217–53; "The Omega Point Theory: A Model for an Evolving God," in *Physics, Philosophy, and Theology*, ed. Robert John Russell (Vatican City: Vatican Observatory, 1988), 313–32; and *Physics of Immortality* (New York: Doubleday, 1994).

6. John Polkinghorne, *Belief in God in an Age of Science* (New Haven, CT: Yale University Press, 1998), ch. 2.

7. John Hick, *An Interpretation of Religion* (New Haven, CT: Yale University Press, 1989), ch. 11.

8. Pierre Teilhard de Chardin, *The Phenomenon of Man* (New York: Harper & Row, 1959).

9. John B. Cobb Jr., *Beyond Dialogue: Toward the Mutual Transformation of Christianity and Buddhism* (Philadelphia: Fortress Press, 1982), ch. 2.

10. John B. Cobb Jr., *Christ in a Pluralistic Age* (Philadelphia: Westminster Press, 1975), 21, 58.

11. According to Kenneth Kraft, *Inner Peace, World Peace: Essays on Buddhism and Nonviolence* (Albany: State University of New York Press, 1992), 18, Thich Nhat Hahn published a book by this title in 1963. While I have not seen this text or any other scholarly reference to it, Christopher S. Queen notes that the French term *engagé*, meaning "politically outspoken" or "politically involved," was common among activist intellectuals in French Indochina long before the 1960s. Queen, "Introduction," in *Engaged Buddhism: Buddhist Liberation Movements in Asia*, ed. Christopher S. Queen and Sallie B. King (Albany: State University of New York Press, 1996), 1–44.

12. Cf. Cobb, *Beyond Dialogue*, chs. 4–5, and John P. Keenan, "Some Questions about the World" and "The Mind of Wisdom and Justice in the Letter of James," in

The Sound of Liberating Truth: Buddhist-Christian Dialogues in Honor of Frederick J. Streng, ed. Sallie B. King and Paul O. Ingram (Surrey: Curzon Press, 1999), 181–99, as two important examples of contemporary Christian dialogue with Buddhists on the relation between nonviolent compassion and love as the center of Christian traditions of social justice.

13. Paul F. Knitter, "Towards a Liberation Theology of Religions," in *The Myth of Christian Uniqueness: Toward a Pluralistic Theology of Religions*, ed. John Hick (Maryknoll, NY: Orbis Books, 1985).

14. Knitter, "Towards a Liberation Theology of Religions," 185–86.

15. Thomas Merton, "Monastic Experience and East-West Dialogue," in *The Asian Journal of Thomas Merton*, ed. Naomi Burton et al. (New York: New Directions Books, 1973), 309–25.

16. "Marxism and Monastic Disciplines," in Burton et al., *The Asian Journal of Thomas Merton* (New York: New Directions Publishing Corporation, 1973), 332–42. Also see Lawrence S. Cunningham, *Thomas Merton and the Monastic Vision* (Grand Rapids, MI: William B. Eerdmans Publishing Company, 1999), 155–82.

17. Cf. Philip Johnston, *Silent Music: The Science of Meditation* (New York: Harper and Row, 1974); Thomas Keating, *Open Mind, Open Heart: The Contemplative Dimension of the Gospel* (New York: Continuum Publications, 1997), and *Invitation to Love: The Way of Christian Contemplation* (New York: Continuum Publications, 1997); also see Thomas Merton, *Mystics and Zen Masters* (New York: Dell Publishing, 1967), and Burton et al., 1973, 211–56, 297–304, 309–17.

18. See Ruben L. F. Habito, *Zen Breath, Healing Breath: Zen Spirituality for a Wounded Earth* (Maryknoll, NY: Orbis Books, 1993), and "The Resurrection of the Dead, and Life Everlasting: From a Futuristic to a Realized Christianity," in King and Ingram, *The Sound of Liberating Truth*, ch. 19.

19. The "cognitive sciences" are a broad collection of disciplines united by a common philosophical perspective and research agenda that includes neuroscience, general psychology, neuropsychology, neurophysiology, cognitive psychology, artificial intelligence, linguistics, anthropology, the study of animal and human intelligence, and (highly speculative) extraterrestrial intelligence. Essentially, any scientific study of the mind, in humans or animals and perhaps in extraterrestrial beings, and its connection with the physiological structures of the brain is a "cognitive science."

~

CHAPTER TWO

Models of Buddhist-Christian Dialogue with the Natural Sciences

Throughout his distinguished career, Ian Barbour has argued that the two most important topics for Christian theological reflection are (1) dialogue with the natural sciences and (2) how the practice of interreligious dialogue might be contextualized by what the natural sciences are discovering about the physical processes structuring the universe. Many Buddhists also conclude that Buddhist interreligious dialogue should be contextualized by scientific accounts of nature. In *Religion and Science*, Barbour discusses four criteria that define successful scientific models and theories that are pertinent to the science-religion dialogue: agreement with data, coherence, scope, and fertility.[1] While these criteria can be employed in analyzing religious models and claims, religious traditions cannot claim to be scientific, "even though they exemplify the same spirit of inquiry found in the standards of science."[2] Theology is critical reflection on the life and thought of various religious communities. Yet, while always revisable, there exist neither controlled experiments nor proofs in theology. Still, there is a process of testing in the experience of a religious community, so that Buddhists and Christians can build cumulative cases from lines of argument. Furthermore, Buddhists and Christians should demand that concepts, doctrines, and models be closely related to the widest body of human experience.

Barbour's discussion of the world's religions in the context of his own particular Christian dialogue with the natural sciences clearly demonstrates the breadth of his thought. Yet, as knowledgeable about the world's religions as Barbour is, the generalist character of his understanding of non-Christian religious traditions has somewhat limited the data, coherence, scope, and fertility of his theological vision. Even so, the very fact that Barbour has acknowledged the need to encounter the natural sciences within the wider contexts of religious pluralism furthers the evolution of current science-religion dialogue. I agree with Barbour on this point and, as a Lutheran Christian, contend that the two most critical areas for contemporary theological reflection are dialogue with the world's religions and dialogue with the natural sciences.

Barbour identifies five features of contemporary scientific thought that constitute a challenge not only to Christian tradition but to all religious traditions: (1) the success of the methods of scientific investigation; (2) the differences between scientific cosmologies and traditional religious cosmologies; (3) the new contexts that science provides for theological reflection on religious understandings of human nature, particularly the doctrine of creation in the monotheistic religions; (4) the fact of religious pluralism, which calls into question the exclusive truth claims of any single religious tradition; and (5) global threats to the environment and the subsequent necessity for religious people to turn toward science to understand the ecological interdependence of all life-forms.[3] Given these challenges, this chapter is based on four assumptions.

First, it seems clear that the natural sciences' revelations about the physical processes at play in the universe have become epistemological models for other disciplines of inquiry. The sciences appear to give us real knowledge of the physical structures of the universe because scientific theories and laws bear some resemblance to the universe they describe That is, they have ontological reference to physical reality.[4] But as John Cobb warns, human beings cannot live by scientific abstractions alone because patterns of scientific abstractions cannot tell us how to constitute ourselves in community with each other and with the other sentient life-forms with which we share this planet.[5] Such issues are the proper focus of Buddhist-Christian reflection in dialogue with the natural sciences.

Second, it is also clear that scientific theories cannot be taken as literal descriptions of the physical universe, as classical realism assumed. Nor are scientific theories merely calculating devices whose only function is to allow the correlation and prediction of experimental observations, as instrumentalism holds. As Barbour notes, most working scientists hold a middle position between classical realism and instrumentalism, which he calls "critical realism": scientific theories and models are "abstract symbol systems, which inadequately and selectively represent particular physical aspects of the world for specific purposes."[6] Critical realism thereby points to a working scientist's real intention while recognizing that scientific theories and models are imaginative human constructs that are always intended to bear ontological correspondence to reality. They are neither literal pictures nor useful fictions, but limited, and revisable, ways of imagining what the physical structures of the universe are. This book appropriates Barbour's understanding of critical realism and its corollary, "inference to the best explanation," as primary epistemological assumptions.[7]

Third, scientific, Buddhist, and Christian truth claims demand response and carry ethical implications for human action. Because science, Buddhism, and Christianity are concerned with the question of truth and how persons should live in accord with truth, neither science nor Buddhism nor Christianity can be ethically neutral. Also, neither science, Buddhism, nor Christianity can attain a completely certain grasp of reality—the way things really are as opposed to the way we wish them to be. Yet, for all three there is reasonable hope for developing approximate understandings of reality. Since truths from different perspectives can never be contradictory, if really true, what the sciences, Buddhism, and Christianity tell us about reality should be capable of synthesis into a wider worldview. Of course, this conclusion cannot be certainly proven, but it is a perspective worth testing by means of Buddhist-Christian interreligious dialogue with the natural sciences as a third partner. I must also admit that my conclusion is a matter of faith, the implications of which are worth exploring. Finally, even if the truths of science, Buddhism, and Christianity can be harmonized into a more general worldview, this does not imply that either the sciences or the traditions of Buddhism and Christianity can be replaced by this worldview.

Fourth, while there are many problems in the overall perspectives that the various natural sciences give us of the physical history of the universe, there exists a surprisingly unified origin narrative starting from Plank time to the present. In broad strokes, as noted in the chapter 1, this narrative claims that 13.5 billion years ago the universe began as an explosion of matter from a singularity that was infinitely small, infinitely hot, and infinitely concentrated outward in all directions to create some hundred billion galaxies, including our galaxy, the Milky Way, which in itself contains billions of stars and our sun and its planets. All things that have existed, now exist, and will ever exist are the interdependent effects of this primal Big Bang.

A metaphysical conclusion I draw from this narrative is grounded in Whiteheadian process philosophy, namely, that the universe is dynamic and open ended, creative of ever new novelty, things and events never before imagined, yet always coming to be in interdependence with what went on before. If this conclusion is valid, it is reasonable to argue that current scientific cosmology provides us with a "metadiscourse" describing the universe by which it is possible to link individual discourses, such as theology, ethics, and politics, or the teachings and practices of Buddhism.

Christian Models of Interaction with the Sciences

The most persuasive description of how Christians have interacted with the natural sciences since the seventeenth century is Ian Barbour's typology. Although a number of Christian theologians and philosophers of science think Barbour's typology needs refining,[8] his is still the most widely accepted starting point for theological reflection on the challenges posed to Christian faith and practice by the natural sciences. Accordingly, I will follow Barbour's typology throughout this book as I compare Christian interaction with the natural sciences with Buddhist forms of interaction, the specifics of which I will describe in the following section. According to Barbour, there are four broad patterns that are the main options that Christians have appropriated in interacting with the natural sciences: conflict, independence, dialogue, and integration.[9]

Conflict

A seventeenth-century example of conflict between science and religion is the case of Galileo, which was partly the result of conditions that no longer exist involving (1) the authority of Aristotle in philosophy, science, and theology; (2) the defensiveness and political power of a Roman Catholic hierarchy that felt threatened by the Protestant Reformation; and (3) Galileo's own lack of political astuteness and tactfulness in his dealing with Pope Urban VIII.[10] The best-known contemporary Christian reaction to Charles Darwin also involves conflict, although the responses of both theologians and scientists in both these examples were, and still are, more diverse than the popular image of "the warfare between science and religion" would lead one to believe. Biblical literalism's response to the natural sciences, particularly the theory of evolution and contemporary cosmology, is the most strident example of theological conflict with the sciences. At the opposite end from biblical literalism is scientific materialism, which has led many prominent scientists to reject all religious claims about the universe.

Both biblical literalism and scientific materialism share several characteristics. Both believe there are serious conflicts between contemporary science and religious beliefs. Both seek certain knowledge, based on logic and sense data in the case of scientific materialism and an infallible scripture in the case of biblical literalism. Both make rival claims about the history of nature, so that one must, both argue, choose between them. Finally, scientific materialism and biblical literalism are, in their own distinctive ways, grounded in philosophical (science) and textual (biblical literalism) reductionism.

Of course, many Christian evangelicals and traditionalists insist on the centrality of Christ without insisting on literal interpretation of an infallible scripture. But radical fundamentalist groups and large portions of major denominations, particularly in the United States—a majority in the case of Southern Baptists—maintain that the Bible is inerrant. This means that biblical literalism is in conflict with contemporary science on several points. First, biblical literalism conflicts with the biological evidence of the evolution of species. Second, it also conflicts with the geological evidence regarding the age of the Earth, which is thought to be approximately 4.5 billion years old, rather than 6,000 years old as biblical literalists assert. Third, it conflicts with physics, according to which the universe originated from a singularity called the Big Bang some 13.5 billion years ago. Fourth, for this reason, biblical literalism conflicts with the simpler and less theoretical facts established by physics, such as that light travels to the Earth from distant galaxies at a constant speed. If the nearest galaxy to the Earth is one or two million light years away, this means that the light from that galaxy has taken one or two million years to travel to the Earth, which makes the idea that the Earth is six thousand years old incoherent.

A more contemporary example of the conflict between biblical literalism and science is the Scopes trial in 1925 in Dayton, Tennessee, where it was successfully argued that the theory of evolution should not be taught in public schools because it was contrary to scripture. More recently, a new fundamentalist claim known as "creation science" has asserted that there is scientific evidence for the creation of the world within the last six thousand years. A law was passed by the Arkansas legislature in 1981 requiring that "creationist theory" be given equal instructional time in public high school biology texts and classes. This law also specified that creationism must be presented as a purely scientific theory with no explicit reference to God. In 1982, the U.S. District Court overturned the Arkansas law because it favored a particular religious view and was therefore in violation of the constitutional separation of church and state. The court also ruled that creation science is not legitimate science and concluded that the scientific community, not a state legislature, the courts, or a particular religious community, should decide the status of scientific theories.

Biblical literalism in all its forms is a thoroughly monological way of interacting with the natural sciences that is a threat to both freedom of religion and scientific freedom. Whenever the absolute claims of a particular religious view are imposed on others in a pluralist society, objections must be made in the name of religious and scientific freedom. But the same can be said for the mirror image of biblical literalism, scientific materialism. Scientific materialists are the intellectual heirs of the materialism of the French Enlightenment, the empiricism of David Hume, and the evolutionary naturalism of the nineteenth century. Most scientific materialists are guided in their understanding of science and religion by two presuppositions: (1) scientific method is the only reliable path to knowledge about all aspects of human experience, and (2) matter-energy is the only fundamental reality in the universe. The first presupposition is an epistemological claim, often referred to as "scientism," and the second is a metaphysical assertion about the nature of ultimate reality foundational to philosophical materialism. These presuppositions are also linked by the assumption that since only the entities and causes disclosed by the natural sciences are real, only the sciences can progressively disclose the nature of reality. Thus, scientific materialism reduces all experience and all reality to the interactions of mechanically understood physical processes.

Of course, science as the source of all that is knowable is the popular image of the sciences in contemporary Western cultures. For example, the physicist Carl Sagan's television series and book, *Cosmos*, is a fascinating summary of recent discoveries and theoretical advances in astronomy, but he interjects his own materialist commentary throughout. Claims such as "the cosmos is the only thing that was, is, or will be" and "the universe is eternal or else it is simply unknowable" run throughout the television series and book.[11] Sagan attacks Christian ideas by arguing that all mystical and authoritarian claims, by which he means religious claims, undercut the scientific method. Nature replaces God in Sagan's cosmology and is his object of reverence. While he sees great beauty in the interrelatedness of the cosmos, expresses deep ethical sensitivity about how humanity should live in the cosmos, for him the universe itself has nothing that transcends it. It just is—in all its beauty and impermanence. His conclusion is that religious apprehensions of a sacred reality that transcends the universe as its creator and sustainer are illusions, ethically dangerous, and barriers to scientific inquiry.

The successes of genetic and molecular biology have also been interpreted as evidence supporting the reductionism of scientific materialism. Francis Crick, codiscoverer of the structure of DNA, has spent his entire professional life defending the claim that the ultimate aim of the biological sciences is to explain all biology in terms of physics and chemistry and that anything not understandable in terms of physics and chemistry is an illusion. Jacques Monod's book on molecular biology, *Chance and Necessity*, is as much a lucid account of molecular biology as it is a spirited defense of scientific materialism.[12] He claims that biology has proven that there is no purpose in nature and that chance alone is the source of all novelty in the biosphere. His thoroughgoing reductionism is evident in his claim that that all living organisms can be reduced to the simple mechanical interactions of molecules. Animals are machines, human beings are machines, consciousness is an illusion, and the realities religious persons experience, like God, are explained away as misinterpretations of biological forces operating blindly and randomly in nature.

Both biblical literalists and scientific materialists fail to recognize the significant differences between scientific and religious assertions. As a methodological practice, scientific method intentionally ignores most features of human experience as it focuses on a very narrow band of physical relationships, thereby excluding from scientific research agendas the distinctive experiences of wider forms of human experience (e.g., aesthetic, moral, and religious experience). However, scientific materialists universalize their judgments about physical relationships to aspects of reality scientific method intentionally ignores. The result is an incoherent promotion of a particular philosophical worldview as if it were a scientific conclusion, just as biblical literalists promote a prescientific cosmology as if it were an essential part of Christian faith, an equally incoherent conclusion. Consequently, dialogue between Buddhism, Christianity, and science becomes impossible.

Independence

It is often asserted that conflict can be avoided if religion and science are understood as two separate enterprises, or "nonoverlapping magisteria," as biologist Stephen Jay Gould phrased the independence model.[13] Each has its own distinctive domain, each is autonomous, each employs its own distinctive methods that can be justified on its own terms, and, therefore, science has nothing to say about religion, nor religion about science. Proponents of this model claim that science and religion are two separate jurisdictions, and each discipline must keep off the turf of the other, keeping to its own business while not meddling in the affairs of the other. This dualistic separation into watertight compartments is motivated by the desire to avoid unnecessary conflict as well as to be faithful to the distinctive character of scientific and religious inquiry.

The two best-known Christian examples of the independence model are Protestant neo-orthodoxy and Protestant existentialist theology. Neo-orthodoxy sought to recover the Reformation emphasis on the centrality of Christ and the primacy of revelation, while fully accepting the results of modern biblical scholarship and scientific research. According to Karl Barth and his followers,[14] God can be known only as revealed in Christ and acknowledge by faith. God is transcendent, wholly other, and unknowable except when disclosed in revelation through Christ. So, the Bible must be taken seriously, but not literally, because the Bible in and of itself is not revelation; nor are the words in the biblical texts "God's words." Here, Barth draws upon St. Augustine: the word of God is Christ through which theology should figure out what the biblical texts mean. Accordingly, while biblical texts must be taken seriously, prescientific biblical views of nature should only be interpreted symbolically. For example, the opening chapters of Genesis should be read as an ancient theological portrayal of the relation between humanity and the world to God, a message about creatureliness, and the goodness of the natural order. In this way, the religious meanings of the biblical texts can be separated from the ancient cosmology through which these meanings are expressed. In this sense, proper Christian faith can in principle have no conflict with the natural sciences.

In theological existentialism, the operating distinction is between the realm of personal selfhood and the realm of impersonal objects. The meaning of personal selfhood is the domain of religion and Christian theological reflection, while the proper domain of the natural sciences is the realm of impersonal natural entities and processes. The operating assumption of theological existentialism is that the meaning of human existence is found only in personal commitment and action, never in the rational methods of scientists searching for abstract general concepts and universal natural laws.

Langdon Gilkey's theology, particularly in his earlier writings, is based squarely on existentialist assumptions rooted in the philosophy of Søren Kierkegaard.[15] According to Gilkey, (1) science seeks to explain objective, public, and repeatable data, while religion asks about the existence of order and beauty in the world and the experiences of our inner life, such as guilt, anxiety, meaninglessness, trust, and wholeness; (2) science is concerned with "how" questions about the physical relationships in the natural order, while religion asks personal "why" questions about, and the origin and destiny of, existence; (3) the authority of the sciences is logical coherence and experimental adequacy, while the final authority in religion is God and revelation understood in personal terms and validated through personal experience; and (4) science makes quantitative predictions that are tested empirically, while religion must employ symbolic and analogical language because sacred realities (God, Emptiness, Brahman, Allah, the Dao) are transcendent to, while immanent within, natural processes and are thereby not accessible to empirical observation and experimentation.

The independence model is also operative in the work of several prominent scientists who are nevertheless very skeptical about the rationality of religious belief. One important example I have noted is Stephen Jay Gould. In his book *Rocks of Ages: Science and Religion in the Fullness of Life,* Gould writes that the idea of a war between science and religion is fundamentally wrong because it fails to account for how science and religion have been historically related, as well as to specify normative arguments for how science and religion ought to be related. He maintains that science and religion frame their own distinctive questions in their own distinctive ways, so that each has its own distinctive criteria for assessing answers to these questions. He writes,

> The net, or magisterium, of science covers the empirical realm: what is the universe made of (fact) and why does it work this way (theory). The magisterium of religion extends over questions of ultimate and moral value. These two magisteria do not overlap, nor do they encompass all inquiry.[16]

It is only when science or religion steps into the territory of the other that there is conflict. In reality, they are independent enterprises and should be understood as "nonoverlapping magisteria." As such, science and religion hold equal worth—in their own separate magisteria. While it is obvious that the conflict model is thoroughly nondialogical, it is equally clear that the independence model also leaves no room for scientific dialogue with Buddhists or Christians. The dualism of nonoverlapping magisteria can only be conducive to monologue.

Dialogue

Dialogue refers to a collection of views that go far beyond the independence model's portrayal of the relationship between science and religion as separate and closed from each other's influence. According to Barbour, the dialogue model focuses on the general characteristics of science and natural processes described by science rather than particular scientific theories. Dialogue is therefore concerned with "limit questions," methodological parallels between science and religion, and nature-centered spiritualities.[17] Limit questions, sometimes called "boundary questions," are metaphysical questions raised by the scientific research but incapable of being answered through the application of scientific method.

The historical contribution of Christian theology (and Islamic *kalam,* or "theology/science") to the origins of modern science in the European Renaissance is well known to theologians, philosophers of science, and historians of science. This fact has led some theologians to conclude that theism is an implicit presupposition or a logical requirement of contemporary science. There is good reason to be skeptical of this claim. Once the natural sciences were established in their own right in separation from Christian medieval theology, beginning in the sixteenth century, the successes of the sciences were sufficient justification for science's conclusions apart from the need for theological justification. Theistic beliefs are not explicit presuppositions of science.

Yet, as wider limit questions are raised by specific conclusions of the sciences, the door seems open to religious answers. Thus, for many scientists, exposure to the order of the universe, as well as its beauty and complexity, engenders a sense of wonder and reverence. This is the view of Thomas Torrance, in company with John Polkinghorne.[18] While maintaining the neo-orthodox distinction between human discovery and divine revelation, Torrance also thinks that science raises fundamental limit questions that science itself cannot answer. For example, as science clearly reveals a natural order that is both rational and contingent because scientific laws and initial conditions were not necessary, it is just as clear that theologians are rationally justified in affirming God as the creator of the contingent, but rational, order of the universe.

Wolfhart Pannenberg has also theologically explored the limit questions of science.[19] He thinks that there are methodological parallels between science and theology in the study of reality as a whole, which means that theologians can use universally rational criteria in parallel with the sciences in studying reality. He views both theology and natural science as "sciences" (wissenschaft), but there is a difference between them. Theology is the "science of God," and its concern is the unique and unrepeatable events in the natural order. These unique and unrepeatable events constitute limit questions not open to scientific investigation. Such limit questions are not about initial conditions or ontological foundations, but about openness toward a future to which God is drawing creation. The sciences are not able to function as a resource for dealing with this specific theological concern.

Physicist-theologian John Polkinghorne is perhaps the best-known contemporary example of an author who invokes methodological parallels between science and religion as an opening for dialogue.[20] His writings focus on the role of personal judgment and the fact that theory-laden data are the justifications for conclusions in both enterprises. He notes that the data for a religious community are its scriptural records and its history of religious experience and that both science and religion are "corrigible," meaning having to relate theory to experience. Furthermore, each field is concerned with entities that are unpicturable and incapable of being accounted for with naive objectivity. Consequently, science has much to learn from theology and theology should be grounded in serious conversation with the natural sciences.

Finally, some writers are drawn into dialogue with the natural sciences by a nature-centered spirituality. For example, Rachael Carson's *Silent Spring* draws from her knowledge of science, but she also professes a strong reverence for the community of living organisms. Loren Eisley was in awe of the interdependence of all living things because of his work as a paleontologist whose science was deeply grounded in evolutionary biology. Both Anne Dillard in *Pilgrim at Tinker Creek* and Aldo Leopold write as a naturalists whose poetic prose portrays a holistic vision of the unity of life. The strong feature of these versions of nature-centered spirituality is their strong emphasis on environmental ethics.

Integration

According to Barbour's typology, a number of contemporary writers seek some sort of integration of the actual content of theology with the actual content of the natural sciences. Here, the relationship between theological doctrines and particular scientific theories is more direct than in the dialogue model. Barbour points to three versions of the integration model: natural theology, theology of nature, and systematic synthesis.

Natural theology has a long and honored history in Christian tradition, as well as in Islamic tradition. Examples include several versions of the cosmological argument for a first cause or a necessary being on whom all contingent beings are dependent. Thomas Aquinas also employed a teleological argument for the existence of God by citing evidence of design in natural phenomena. Isaac Newton, Robert Boyle, Gottfried Leibniz, and other key figures in the origins of modern science often cited the orderliness of nature as evidence of God as a benevolent designer. And while David Hume strongly criticized such design arguments, they were still popular in the nineteenth century, particularly in the form design arguments assumed in the natural theology of William Paley. After the publication of Darwin's *Origin of Species* in 1859, design arguments meant to demonstrate the existence of God fell out of favor in mainline Protestant and liberal Catholic theology.

Some current strands of natural theology point to the "anthropic principle" as an argument for the reasonableness of belief in the existence of God. The anthropic principle was developed in several versions, but the main thrust is that life in the universe would have been impossible if the physical constants in nature had differed even slightly from the values they have. Seen from this perspective, the universe seems "fine-tuned" for the possibility of life. For example, Stephen Hawking notes that if the rate of expansion one second after the Big Bang had been smaller by even one part in a hundred thousand million million million, the universe would have recollapsed into itself shortly after it began expanding from its initial singularity.[21] While Hawking does not employ the fine-tuning of the universe as an argument for the existence of God, Freeman Dyson thinks the universe's fine-tuning is most coherently explained by the hypothesis that mind, perhaps God's mind, plays an creative role in the universe's physical processes. He writes,

> I conclude from the existence of these accidents of physics and astronomy that the universe is an unexpectedly hospitable place for living creatures to make their home in. Being a scientist, trained in the habits of thought and language of the twentieth century rather than the eighteenth, I do not claim that the architecture of the universe *proves* the existence of God. I claim only that the architecture of the universe is consistent with the hypothesis that mind plays an essential role in its functioning.[22]

Unlike natural theology, a theology of nature does not start from science but from the "data" of religious experience, doctrine, and, in Christian and Islamic traditions, revelation. Consequently, while theology of nature generally affirms that some traditional doctrines should be reformulated in light of current understandings of physical processes, science and religion are normally understood as relatively independent enterprises, but with some areas of overlapping concern. In Christian tradition in particular, the doctrines of creation, providence, and human nature are reformulated in light of the discoveries of the natural sciences. Thus, while some religious beliefs and practices are said to be in harmony with scientific knowledge, modifications of some traditional Christian doctrines are necessary because our understanding of natural processes at work in nature will necessarily constrain our understanding of God's relation to the natural order and the role of humanity in this order. The problem of evil will also be given much attention in view of the role of natural selection in the origins and evolution of all life-forms.

For biochemist and theologian Arthur Peacocke, the starting point of theological reflection was the past and present religious experience of a religious community.[23] Religious beliefs are tested by community consensus, comprehensiveness, and fruitfulness in the lives of those who participate in the community. But Peacocke also thought that traditional religious beliefs need reformulation in response to current science. His particular theological reflection was an extended discussion of how chance and necessity work independently together in the cosmos, quantum physics, nonequilibrium thermodynamics, and biological evolution and how specific Christian doctrines should be revised accordingly. Peacocke claimed that God creates through the whole process of chance and necessity, not by intervening in gaps in this process. "God of the gaps" must by all means be avoided, so that, for Peacocke, God creates "in, with, and under" the processes of natural systems.

The writings of Pierre Teilhard de Chardin also exemplify a theology of nature approach to the natural sciences.[24] Teilhard, a Jesuit and a paleontologist, was deeply formed by his Roman Catholic heritage and Jesuit spirituality. Yet, he modified his concept of God in light of the theory of evolution. Thus, he wrote of an ongoing process of creation and a God immanent in an unfinished universe. His vision of a final convergence of existence into an "Omega point" is a speculative theological extrapolation of evolutionary directionality filtered through the lenses of Christian eschatology.

The final form of the integration model, systematic synthesis, occurs when both science and religion contribute to a coherent general worldview elaborated through a comprehensive metaphysics. Metaphysics is a form of philosophical reflection that searches for a set of general explanatory categories in terms of which the totality of experience can be interpreted. For example, Aquinas, by appropriating Aristotle's substance metaphysics, sought to unify knowledge of both nature and God in a *summa*, or "summary," of what human beings can know of God and nature. The most promising contemporary form of the integration model, at least to my mind, is process philosophy, particularly the form of process thought originating with Alfred North Whitehead and Charles Hartshorne, both of whose philosophies were directly influenced by relativity theory, quantum theory, and the theory of evolution.[25] Process theologians and philosophers understand God to be the source of novelty and order in the universe through a creative process that is incomplete and, therefore, ongoing.

Change, chance, novelty, and order characterize the structure of nature according to process theology, and the role of physics and biology is evident in process thought's understanding of this structure. God, for process theologians, is understood to be the source for both novelty and order. Creation is a long and incomplete process through which God elicits novelty, as well as order and structure. God is not an unrelated absolute or an unmoved mover, but interacts reciprocally with every thing and event in the world at every moment of space-time—past, present, and future—because God is an influence on all events, though never the sole cause of any event. So, God transcends the universe while remaining immanent within the natural processes of the universe. This implies the rejection of God's omnipotence, a classical Christian doctrine replaced in process theology by the notion that God interacts with all events in creation through persuasion, rather than compulsion.

Biologist Charles Birch and theologian John Cobb, in *The Liberation of Life*, integrate the biological sciences, Whiteheadian process metaphysics, and Christian theological tradition in a way that is typical of process thought. In their view, (1) every living being is constituted by its interaction with the wider environment of which it is a part, and (2) all living entities are subjects of experience, which run the gamut from unconscious stimulus-response reactions to reflective self-consciousness. Evolutionary history demonstrates that there is both continuity and the emergence of novelty, and humanity is a continuous part of this evolutionary process. Accordingly, Birch and Cobb develop an ethic centering on "the liberation of life" that avoids anthropocentricism, the goal of which is enhancing the richness of experience of all living organisms, human and nonhuman—as much as this is possible in a world where life must eat life to survive.

In my own reflection on the interaction between the natural sciences and Christian theological reflection, Barbour's integration model has proven to be the most fruitful option. But, while I also think that a systematic metaphysics like Whitehead's and Hartshorne's can guide reflective Christians to a more coherent vision of reality, I nevertheless do not think that Christian faith should be equated with any metaphysical system or scientific theory. The danger is that when either scientific or religious ideas are distorted to fit a preconceived synthesis that claims to encompass all of reality, both scientific conclusions and theological conclusions become incoherent. The richness and diversity of experience simply transcends metaphysical reductionism. The clue here is Whitehead himself, who wrote that any metaphysical scheme, like any scientific theory or theological vision, is always subject to revision according to new experiences and theoretical insight. In light of this, critical realism seems the most appropriate epistemological stance.

Buddhist Models of Interaction with Science

In some ways, Buddhist typologies describing the interaction between science and religion are similar to Barbour's, but Buddhists add their own distinctive perspectives. The clearest description of the typologies according to which Buddhists have engaged the sciences is that of José Ignacio Cabezón.[26] As with Barbour's typology, Cabezón's is historical in intent because he focuses on the actual forms of interaction between Buddhism and the natural sciences, which he names (1) conflict/ambivalence, (2) compatibility/identity, and (3) complementarity.

Conflict/Ambivalence

According to Cabezón,

> Today there is certainly to be found in the literature what might be considered anti-Buddhist sentiments on the part of scientists, but this is usually not directed specifically at Buddhism, being instead a part of more general antireligious sentiments that are found on naive mechanistic materialism. Likewise, there is a good deal of skepticism on the part of Buddhists as regards, for example, some of the technological fruits of science, but this critique falls short of a full-blown repudiation of science.[27]

Cabezón's assessment points to the fact that the sciences, especially when represented through the filter of materialism, have presented somewhat different challenges for Christians than for Buddhists. I shall compare and contrast these challenges, along with challenges posed to both Buddhism and Christianity by conclusions generally accepted in scientific cosmology, evolutionary theory, and neuroscience that are *not* read through the lenses of materialism in subsequent chapters of this book. At this juncture, what requires clarification is that Christians and Buddhists do not interact with the natural sciences in identical ways in spite of areas of similarity. Christian experiences with the natural sciences are not identical to Buddhist experiences.

It is clear that conflict with the sciences has occurred in Buddhism, but not to the degree it has in Christian tradition. In fact, Cabezón thinks conflict is relatively absent among Buddhists.[28] Conflict, where it has existed, is normally not outright antagonism but takes the form of mutual disregard, or, when science and Buddhism have actually engaged one other, ambivalence. Where outright conflict has existed, it occurred mostly in Asia, where the sciences were first perceived as the source of the power of European colonialism. Since European colonialism was the earliest vehicle by which Western science was introduced into Asian cultures, Asian opposition to colonialism, its earliest phases at least, included rejection of science. Generally speaking, however, some Asian Buddhist views of the natural sciences are best characterized as ambivalent. For example, in Tibet before the 1959 invasion of the Chinese, there was widespread skepticism about science among the Buddhist monastic leadership, who tended to interpret science and technology as part of a Western colonial ideology that threatened to undermine Buddhism and monastic control of the state. Yet, there were individuals, for example, the current Dalai Lama and other prominent Tibetan intellectuals, who developed considerable interest in the sciences. These individuals were able to distinguish between science and Western colonial political ideology and, thereby, did not apprehend science as a threat to Buddhism as such.

This pattern of relationship with the natural sciences existed in other parts of the Buddhist world and is best characterized as ambivalence rather than outright rejection. At the same time, in the same cultures, other Buddhists leaders took a more open approach to science and technology as part of their support for modernizing their countries guided by Buddhist ethical values.

If some Buddhist attitudes toward science can be characterized as ambivalent, most working scientists are not interested in Buddhism. Anti-Buddhist sentiments among a few scientists do exist, but they are usually not specifically directed toward Buddhism as such; rather, they are part of a more general criticism of all forms of religion because of the materialistic assumptions of some scientists. Most scientists and Buddhists continue merely to ignore each other, although in the last few decades there has emerged an important dialogue between the two. This dialogue is best characterized as either compatibility/identity or complementarity.

Compatibility/Identity

When two different cultures or religious traditions first encounter one another, the first reaction is usually to treat the culturally or religiously other in terms of the culturally or religiously familiar. This was the usual pattern when Buddhism and Western science first began to interact in the eighteenth century. It is also a pattern that continues into the present, where the focus is on similarity. Of course, there exist degrees of compatibility ranging from what Cabezón calls "complementarity"—the claim that Buddhism and science are similar because they share common concerns, reach similar conclusions, and employ similar empirical methods—to identity. Identity is the stronger claim that Buddhism *is* a science, or at least "scientific," because the objects of Buddhist investigation and the results, aims, and methods of Buddhist meditation are fully empirical and, therefore, "scientific."[29]

One of the earliest Western Buddhists to explore the relation between Buddhism and science was Henry Steel Olcott in his *A Buddhist Catechism*, which was first published at the end of the nineteenth century.[30] His view is that Buddhism and science are complementary. Inspired by Western enlightenment assumptions, Olcott claims that Buddhism and science are in essential agreement about the nature of reality for two reasons: (1) both teach evolution because both see human development emerging through different stages, from imperfect lower beings to higher conditions and states of existence; and (2) both teach that all things and events are subject to universal laws, in Buddhism called the laws of karma and samsara and in science called

Newton's laws of motion. So, according to Olcott, Buddhism and science are in agreement because both assert the existence of natural laws governing the evolution of both human beings and the universe as such. Still, Olcott remains somewhat ambivalent about the natural sciences. Although Buddhism encourages the teaching of science, science is not a moral philosophy, as is Buddhism, since Buddhism does not waste time speculating about the origins of things. Here, Olcott asserts the authority of the Buddha, who, it is said in the Pali Canon, labeled questions of origins as "speculative" and "not suitable for the achievement of Awakening" (*nibbāna*, in Sanskrit, *nirvāṇa*).[31]

Another early example of compatibility is the view of Anagarika Dharmapala, a Sri Lankan Buddhist in attendance at the first World Parliament of Religions in Chicago in 1893. He typifies a major theme of nineteenth-century Buddhist reformers who sought to free their societies from European colonialism: Buddhism, not Christianity, can heal the breach between science and religion.[32] Paul Carus, an American editor, publisher, and advocate of Buddhist monasticism, also believed that Buddhism could be reconciled with science, which implied for him the superiority of Buddhism to Christianity.[33] D. T. Suzuki was of the same opinion in his view of Zen tradition, which he asserted is the essence of the Buddha's teachings and practice, a point he, like Carus, also argued at the World Parliament of Religions. These examples of compatibility have a common argument, namely, that Buddhism is in accordance with the discoveries of science in both content and conclusions because Buddhism has always embraced the importance of a scientific outlook. Furthermore, the empirical nature of Buddhist meditative practice seemed to both Suzuki and Carus to be similar to the empirical nature of scientific method. Accordingly, the doctrines of Buddhism are capable of empirical verification in a way that the teachings of Christian tradition are not. But compatibility/identity is not a relic of the eighteenth century because this model is assumed by many contemporary Buddhist teachers and practitioners. Even a scholar as knowledgeable as Hubert Guenther claims that Buddhism is scientific in its premises and worldview.[34] The rhetoric of identity is also very much alive in the work of Gerald Du Pre, who writes that scientific psychology was not created by Wilhelm Wundt and Sigmund Freud, "but two thousand five hundred years earlier in India, by Prince Siddhartha."[35]

Complementarity

Similar to Barbour's conflict model, conflict/ambivalence assumes there exist differences between science and religion that are ultimately irreconcilable. Opposite to this, compatibility/identity asserts a fundamental similarity between the natural sciences and Buddhism's worldview, while in its extreme form this model asserts an actual identity between science and Buddhism's worldview. Cabezón argues that complementarity lies between the "extremes" of conflict/ambivalence and similarity/identity because this model focuses on negotiating both similarities and differences.[36] Accordingly, the rhetoric of this model usually asserts similarity of methods but difference in objects of investigation. Thus, Buddhism is portrayed as an interior science, or a science of mind, that engenders a "technology of spirit" identified with the practice of meditation, while the sciences are concerned with the objective physical processes of nature. So, while there are differences in *what* Buddhism and science investigate, the claim is that both are similar in *how* they investigate their respective objects. Consequently, Buddhism and science are interdependent parts of a greater whole (e.g., Buddhism is experiential, science is experimental; Buddhism investigates the mind; science investigates matter; Buddhism is qualitative, science is quantitative; Buddhism is contemplative, science is conventional). Finally, it is often argued that Buddhism actually benefits from the facts about the material world revealed by the sciences, facts that historically have not been part of traditional Buddhist speculations about nature.

Victor Mansfield, who is both a Buddhist and a physicist, is an important contemporary example of the complementarity between science and Buddhism, in his case a Tibetan form of Madhyamika, or "middle way," Buddhism, founded in the second century BC by Buddhist logician Nagarjuna. But in Mansfield's case, it is not just that Buddhism and science employ similar methods or reach identical conclusions. Each has implications for the other that, when recognized, can yield greater insight into both Buddhism and the natural sciences.[37] Likewise, Robert Thurman argues that while science is concerned with exploration of the material universe, Buddhism is concerned with developing an "inner science." So, whereas the natural sciences—psychology and neuropsychology—concern themselves with the biological process and the "hard wiring" of the brain, Tibetan Buddhist styles of meditation are "mind sciences" that provide humanity with the "software" for understanding and modifying the mind.[38] A final example is the work of Daniel Goldman, who, while recognizing similarities in content between Western and Buddhist psychology, concludes that these similarities are merely "surface" similarities. For him, the complementarity of the methods of Buddhism and science should be the focus of Buddhist-science dialogue.[39]

However, not all Buddhists engaged in dialogue with the natural sciences, even when both are understood to be complementary, are convinced about the existence of a common structure that can unify the sciences and Buddhism. One such scholar is Cabezón:

I remain unconvinced about such a common structure, just as I remain unconvinced that the various "conventional" psychological schemes of human development can be harmonized into a unified and consistent template that would be acceptable to each of the Western *theorists*. . . . Equally problematic is the tendency . . . to ascribe to the contemplative traditions a lack of thematization concerning the *conventional* workings of the mind and the conventional self.[40]

The question is whether the conclusion that Buddhism and science (or any religion and science) share a common structure has validity. How could this be determined in a way that would satisfy either a practicing Buddhist or a skeptical scientist (unless, of course, one were a practicing Buddhist already convinced for religious reasons that such a common structure indeed exists)? It may be true that science and Buddhism share a common structure, but it also may not be true. Either way, science as such can offer no supporting arguments. So, perhaps, speaking as a non-Buddhist, the better approach is to assume that while no truth can ultimately contradict any other truth, if it is really true, it might be best to concentrate on the ways that science and Buddhism can creatively transform one another apart from the assumption of a common structure or a common method of investigation which they apply to different objects. There is always a possibility that scientific conclusions regarding natural process will contradict Buddhist experience and doctrines, as well as Christian experience and doctrines, and that Buddhists and Christians will need to make adjustments accordingly.

For this reason, I recommend the adoption of what Barbour calls "critical realism": scientific, Christian, or Buddhist conclusions and practices are intended to correspond to reality—the way things really are—but in principle can only do so provisionally and, therefore, are always in need of reformulation. Neither science, Buddhism, nor Christianity possesses the final truth about the natural order or ultimate reality. This reason alone provides justification for Buddhist-Christian-science dialogical engagement. What such dialogue requires is some form of mutual critical integration among the sciences, Buddhism, and Christianity that recognizes the distinctive character of each expression of the search for truth but does not reduce science to either Buddhism or Christianity or to claims that Buddhism and Christianity is "scientific."

Notes

1. Ian G. Barbour, *Religion and Science: Historical and Contemporary Issues* (San Francisco: Harper San Francisco, 1997), 113, 158–59.

2. Barbour, *Religion and Science*, 159.

3. Barbour, *Religion and Science*, xii–xv.

4. Barbour, *Religion and Science*, 117–19.

5. John B. Cobb Jr., "Global Theology in a Pluralistic Age," in *Transforming Christianity and the World*, ed. Paul F. Knitter (Maryknoll, NY: Orbis Books, 1999), 53.

6. Barbour, *Religion and Science*, 106–10.

7. "Inference to the best explanation" refers to how scientists generally decide between two or more theoretical explanations of the same range of data. For example, Charles Darwin's approach in arguing for his theory of evolution through natural selection was to compare two rival explanations of the broad range of available evidence and to show how well each theory's hypotheses explained that evidence. These rival hypotheses to his theory of natural selection and the theory of special creation are centered on the idea that each species was created in its final form. Darwin's "inference to the best explanation" demonstrated that natural selection is a better explanation of the evidence. See Phil Dowe, *Galileo, Darwin, and Hawking* (Grand Rapids, MI: William B. Eerdmans Publishing Company, 2005), 118–24.

8. See, for example, Mikael Stenmark, *How to Relate Science and Religion* (Grand Rapids, MI: William B. Eerdmans Publishing Company, 2004), 250–59, and Christian Berg, "Barbour's Way(s) of Relating Science and Theology," in *Fifty Years in Science and Religion: Ian G. Barbour and His Legacy*, ed. Robert John Russell (Burlington VT: Ashgate Publishing, 2004), 61–75.

9. See Barbour, *Religion and Science*, ch. 4, for a fuller description of these four types.

10. See John Hedley Brooke, *Science and Religion: Some Historical Perspectives* (Cambridge: Cambridge University Press, 1991), 99–116.

11. Carl Sagan, *Cosmos* (New York: Random House: 1980), 4.

12. Jacques Monod, *Chance and Necessity* (New York: Vintage Books, 1972), 180.

13. Stephen Jay Gould, *Rocks of Ages: Science and Religion in the Fullness of Life* (New York: Ballantine, 1999).

14. A good introduction is Karl Barth, *Dogmatics in Outline* (New York: Harper and Row, 1949). Also see W. A. Whitehouse, *Christian Faith and the Scientific Attitude* (New York: Philosophical Library, 1952), for a summary of neo-orthodoxy's theological understanding of science.

15. Langdon Gilkey, *Creationism on Trial* (Minneapolis: Winston Press, 1985), and *Religion and the Scientific Future* (New York: Harper and Row, 1970), ch. 2.

16. Gould, *Rocks of Ages*, 58.

17. Barbour, *Religion and Science*, 90.

18. Thomas Torrance, "God and the Contingent World," *Zygon* 14 (1979): 347.

19. Wolfhart Pannenberg, *Theology and the Philosophy of Science* (Philadelphia, PA: Westminster Press, 1976), ch. 5.

20. John Polkinghorne, *Belief in God in an Age of Science* (New Haven, CT: Yale University Press, 1998), ch. 2.

21. Stephen Hawking, *A Brief History of Time* (New York: Bantam Books, 1988), 291.

22. Freeman Dyson, *Disturbing the Universe* (New York: Harper and Row, 1979), 291, emphasis supplied. Cited in Barbour, *Religion and Science*, 100.

23. Arthur Peacocke, *Theology for a Scientific Age* (Minneapolis: Fortress Press, 1993), 1–24.

24. Pierre Teilhard de Chardin, *The Phenomenon of Man* (New York: Harper & Row, 1959), and *The Future of Man* (New York: Harper & Row, 1959).

25. Alfred North Whitehead, *Process and Reality*, corrected edition by David Ray Griffin and Donald W. Swinburne (1929; repr., New York: Free Press, 1978), and Charles Hartshorne, *The Divine Relativity* (New Haven, CT: Yale University Press, 1948).

26. José Ignacio Cabezón, "Buddhism and Science: On the Nature of the Dialogue," in *Buddhism and Science: Breaking New Ground*, ed. B. Alan Wallace (New York: Columbia University Press, 2003), 35–68.

27. Cabezón, "Buddhism and Science," 43.

28. Cabezón, "Buddhism and Science," 41.

29. Cabezón, "Buddhism and Science," 43–44.

30. Henry Steel Olcott, *A Buddhist Catechism According to the Singhalese Canon* (London: Allen, Scott, 1889).

31. Olcott also believed that "occult science" had substantiated claims of spiritualism, telepaths, and others who had experienced similar phenomena. He was also disappointed by the rejection of such beliefs by science. See Thomas Tweed, *The American Encounter with Buddhism, 1844–1912* (Bloomington: Indiana University Press, 1992), 110.

32. Tweed, *American Encounter*, 103–105.

33. Tweed, *American Encounter*, 105–106.

34. H. V. Guenther, *Matrix of Mystery: Scientific and Humanistic Aspects of rDzogs-chen Thought* (Boston: Shambala, 1984), 98–99.

35. Gerald Du Pre, "The Buddhist Philosophy of Science," in *Buddhism and Science*, ed. B. P. Kirtisinghe (Delhi: Motilal Press, 1984), 110, cited in Cabezón, "Buddhism and Science," 48.

36. Cabezón, "Buddhism and Science," 49.

37. Victor Mansfield, "Time in Madhyamika Buddhism and Modern Physics," *The Pacific World* 11–12 (1995–1996).

38. Robert A. Thurman, *Inner Revolution: Life, Liberty, and the Pursuit of Real Happiness* (New York: Riverhead, 1998), 275.

39. Daniel Goldman and Robert A. Thurman, *Mind Science: An East-West Dialogue* (Boston: Wisdom, 1991), 100–101.

40. Cabezón, "Buddhism and Science," 53.

CHAPTER THREE

~

The Challenge of
Contemporary Cosmology[1]

In the preface to his Terry lectures, John Polkinghorne argues from his perspective as a physicist that there is no a priori reason that

> scientific theories and models and beautiful equations should prove to be the clue to understanding nature; why fundamental physics should be possible; why our minds have such ready access to the deep structure of the universe. It is a contingent fact that this is true of us and of our world, but it does not seem sufficient simply to regard it as a happy accident. Surely it is a significant insight into the nature of reality.

But as a Christian theologian, he concludes,

> I believe that Dirac and Einstein, making their great discoveries, were participating in an encounter with the divine. . . . There is much more to the Mind of God than physics will ever disclose, but this usage is not misleading, for I believe that the rational beauty of the cosmos reflects the Mind that brings it into being. . . . I do not present this conclusion as a logical demonstration—we are in a realm of metaphysical discourse where such certainty is not available either to believer or unbeliever—but I do present it as a coherent and intellectually satisfying understanding.[2]

From my perspective as a Lutheran Christian, I agree with Polkinghorne. Yet, I am more certain about the nature of the theological challenges and positive contributions of dialogue with the natural sciences to Christian faith and practice than I am of the contributions dialogue with the sciences might make to Buddhist faith and practice. It's not just that Buddhists need to decide this question for themselves. Most Buddhists now writing about the natural sciences seem to agree that standard Buddhist doctrines are supported, rather than challenged, by the natural sciences. But Buddhism is a nontheistic religious tradition and, therefore, might be strong evidence against my thesis that the natural sciences provide a common origin narrative that can be appropriated by Buddhists *and* Christians.

The Challenge to Christian Tradition

Since Christian monotheism and Buddhist nontheism seem so incommensurable, further reflection on the current scientific origin narrative that both Christians and Buddhists now share will serve as an illustration of my dilemma. According to this narrative, a plausible reconstruction of cosmic history has emerged that is widely accepted in its general details by the scientific community. Some 13.5 billion years ago, the contents of the universe were together in an initial singularity, meaning a region of infinite curvature and energy density at which the known laws of physics break down ($t = 0$).[3] There was a big bang. The history of the cosmos began some three minutes after this event, when protons and neutrons were combining to form nuclei. Five hundred thousand years later, atoms were coming into existence. One billion years from $t = 0$, galaxies and stars were being formed, followed by planets at ten billion years. At four billion years after $t = 0$, the Earth was forming, along with the other planets in our solar system. After another one billion years, microscopic forms of life were beginning to appear on the Earth.

The farther back we go beyond the first three minutes, the more tentative Big Bang theories become because cosmologists must deal with states of matter and energy increasingly far from anything physicists can at present experimentally duplicate in the laboratory.[4] Protons and neutrons form from their constituent quarks at 10^{-4} seconds (one ten thousandth of a second from $t = 0$), when the temperature of the universe had cooled to 10^{12} degrees (a thousand billion degrees). This sea of hot quarks would have formed at about 10^{-10} seconds from an even smaller and hotter fireball. According to the inflationary theories proposed by Alan Guth and Andrae Linde, the universe underwent a very rapid expansion at about 10^{-35} seconds due to the tremendous energy released in the breaking of symmetry when the strong force separated from the other forces (the weak force, gravity, and the electromagnetic force).[5] In that instant, microscopic fluctuations in the density of the universe, expanding from subatomic scales to the size of a grapefruit in less than a trillionth of a second, were greatly amplified to emerge ultimately into the incredible tapestry of stars and galaxies that now fill the universe. Before 10^{-35} seconds, temperatures would have been so hot that all the forces except gravity were of comparable strength. Physicists have almost no idea about events before $t = 10^{-43}$ (Plank time), when the temperature was about 10^{32} degrees, and the universe was about the size of an atom with an incredible density of 10^{96} times that of water.

If this origin narrative is accurate, it seems reasonable to ask what caused the Big Bang. The Christian (and Islamic and Jewish) answer is that God created the universe and that God could do so through initiating the Big Bang. But there is a problem with the Christian doctrine of creation that seems, at first glance, to point in the direction of Buddhist nontheism. The problem is that cosmologists claim that the Big Bang marked not only beginning of the universe but also the start of time. Time did not exist before the Big Bang, so there could have been no cause of the Big Bang. "What place then for a creator?" asks Stephen Hawking in A *Brief History of Time*,[6] to which one might add, "or divine agency in the continuing processes of nature?"

The Buddhist answer to Hawking's question is that there is no place for a creator or for divine agency. Nontheism has always been the center the Buddhist worldview. So, Buddhists like Geoffrey Redmond argue that scientific cosmology readily harmonizes with Buddhism since Buddhism's traditional cosmology can be construed as a metaphor without "weakening the Buddhist edifice." Furthermore, Redmond argues, cosmology never had the centrality that creation has in Christian and Jewish tradition. "Buddhism never committed itself to a particular ontology," he writes, "which could be contradicted by modern psychological or anthropological conceptions of such beliefs as metaphorical or archetypal."[7] Therefore, "Buddhism is closer to science than is revealed religion in the way it seeks truth."[8]

Of course, the challenge of Big Bang cosmology to the Christian doctrine of creation became crystal clear as this cosmology won wide acceptance beginning in the 1960s. For example, one way theologians have responded is by reflecting on the relation between space and time in the scientific origin narrative. As I as understand this narrative, the Big Bang was an unusual explosion because it did not take place at a particular location in space. This means there existed no space outside the Big Bang. A common analogy to imagine this conclusion is a rubber balloon onto which are glued a number of coins. The coins represent galaxies. As air is pumped into the balloon, it expands. Suppose a fly were to land on one of the coins. What would it see? All the other coins moving away from it, which is, of course, the observed motion of the galaxies relative to scientists studying them from Earth.

Astronomers now think the motion of the galaxies is due to the space between galaxies' expanding, rather than the galaxies' moving through space. In other words, the galaxies are being carried outward from the singularity of the Big Bang on a tide of expanding space, just as coins glued to a balloon are carried apart by its rubber as the balloon expands. Furthermore, just as there is no empty stretch of rubber surface "outside" the region where the coins are clued, so there is no empty three-dimensional space outside where galaxies are to be found. It is this interpretation of the recession of the galaxies that leads cosmologists to conclude that all space that now exists was squashed to an infinitesimal singularity at the Big Bang. In other words, space began as nothing and has continued expanding ever since.

There is also an even more extraordinary element in this cosmology. According to Albert Einstein's theory of general relativity, space and time are welded together into a four-dimensional continuum called "space-time." One cannot have space without time or time without space. In Buddhist language, they are "co-originated," meaning "interdependent." This being so, the Big Bang marked not only the coming into existence of space but also the beginning of time. This means that just as there is no space before the Big Bang, there is also no time before the Big Bang.

It is this aspect of contemporary scientific cosmology that many Buddhists believe gets rid of the sort of creator God that most people have in mind when they think of the Genesis creation story: a God who first exists alone and then decides to create the universe. God says some words, there is a big bang, and Wham! creation begins. Indeed, if the word "God" refers to this sort of entity, Buddhist nontheism seems more closely allied with current scientific cosmology than Christian monotheism.

However, much depends on the meaning of the word "God." Consider the following quotation from St. Augustine:

> It is idle to look for time before creation, as if time can be found before time. If there were no motion of either a spiritual or corporal creature by which the future, moving through the present, would succeed the past, there would be no time at all. We should therefore say that time began with creation, rather than creation began with time.[9]

In other words, for God, there is neither before nor after; God simply *is* in a motionless eternity. Time and space are part of creation. Before creation, there is neither time nor space and, therefore, literally "nothing."[10] Deeply influenced by Platonic ideas, Augustine could write as early as his *Confessions*, "It is not in time that you [God] precede all times; all your 'years' subsist in simultaneity, because they do not change; your 'years' are 'one day' and your today is eternity."[11]

So, Augustine argues, we know time exists because things change—in Buddhist language, all things change because all things are impermanent. If nothing changed, if nothing "moved" in Augustine's language, we could not distinguish one point in time from another, and there would be no way of determining to what the word "time" referred. Accordingly, Augustine argues, if there were no objects that change, that is, "move," there would be no objects at all. "Time" would be a meaningless category. Furthermore, if there is no time, there is no space ("either") through which objects move or that they occupy. In other words, no moving objects, no time; no time, no space.[12]

In this way, Augustine's theology of creation distinguishes between ontological and historical origination, and he concludes that time and space are as much a property of the universe as anything else, and it makes no sense to think of God's predating the creation of the universe. Yet, none of this has an adverse affect on Augustine's theology because he notes that there is an important distinction between the words "creation" and "origins." While in everyday conversations, we might use these words interchangeably, in Christian theological discourse since Augustine, each word has its own distinctive meaning. For example, if one has in mind a question like, how did the universe begin, one is asking a question about historical "origins." Questions of origins are empirical matters for scientists to decide, their current research pointing to the Big Bang cosmology.

The question of "creation" poses ontological issues that are different from the question of the universe's historical "origins." In Christian teaching, "creation" has as much to do with the present instant of time as any other instant of time. Why is there something and not nothing? Why are we here? To whom or to what do we owe our existence? What keeps us in existence? Thus, Christian theological reflection on creation concerns the underlying "ground" of all things and events in space-time, past, present, and future. On the other hand, the question of the universe's origins has to do with what started the physical processes that ended up as the universe.

Ian Barbour continues Augustine's line of argument in his interpretation of the doctrine of creation *ex nihilo* in light of Big Bang cosmology. In *Religion and Science*, he makes as sharp a distinction between ontological/historical categories as Langdon Gilkey makes in *Maker of Heaven and Earth*[13] (which is a contemporary neo-orthodox restatement of Augustine's distinctions). According to Barbour, creation is an ontological issue and is the central meaning of "ex nihilo," or "out of nothing," while $t = 0$ in Big Bang theory is an empirical issue and plays no role in the doctrine of creation *ex nihilo.*[14] Accordingly, Barbour thinks it wise that theologians not employ Big Bang cosmology as a means of demonstrating the reasonableness of theism. However, in his criticism of Barbour's position, physicist-theologian Robert John Russell reports that should an initial singularity ($t = 0$) be supported scientifically, Barbour believes this *would* provide an "impressive example of dependence on God."[15] Russell also notes that the inclusion of a marginal significance of $t = 0$ in Barbour's theology represents something of a shift in his thought. Nevertheless, Barbour continues to distinguish sharply between ontological and historical origins and places most of the theological weight of his theology on the ontological interpretation of the universe's creation, with "only nodding attention to the possibility of the historical interpretation being relevant."[16]

The point of the foregoing discussion is to show that questions about the universe's ontological or historical origins are seen by Buddhists as posing no significant challenges to Buddhist thought and practice. In fact, contemporary Buddhist writers tend to dismiss origin questions as meaningless. In traditional Buddhist cosmology, the universe is portrayed as an eternally changing system of interdependent interrelationships without beginning or end. Contemporary Western Buddhists especially think we should simply accept the universe as a brute fact and ask what, if anything, is gained by affirming that God created it. For Buddhists, the Christian doctrine of creation not only raises the question of who created God; it also implies that any notion of divine creation encourages clinging (*taṇhā*) to an imagined permanent, sacred reality. The karmic result of such clinging to imagined permanent realities can only be suffering (*duḥkha*).[17]

From a Christian perspective, however, Buddhist criticism of Christian notions of creation often misinterprets how mainline Christian theology uses the word "God." For example, Paul Tillich appropriated Augustine's notions of time when he wrote that God is not an "existent object or being."[18] In other words, one cannot say that "God exists" in the same way that one can say "apples exist," or for that matter, "the universe exists." The point of the Christian doctrine of creation is that God is the source of all existence; "God" is the name Christians (and Jews and Muslims) give to whatever is responsible for the existence of all space-time things and events, including human beings. However, most Buddhist interpretations of the Christian doctrine of creation mistakenly assume that Christians affirm God as an object confined within the limits of space and time or that God can only exist "in time." Certainly, one hears such theological talk among some conservative evangelical and fundamentalist Christians. But the mainline teaching is that while we experience God in time and space, God is not confined by time and space.

An emerging question now seems clear: if none of the challenges posed to the themes of traditional Christian theism—here illustrated by the doctrine of God as creator, both "in the beginning" and continually in the present—seemingly pose serious challenges to Buddhism's nontheistic worldview, how can Buddhist faith and practice be creatively transformed through conceptual dialogue with Christian theology mediated by the sciences as a "third party"? Reflection on this question will require a brief description of the sorts of conversations with physicists and cosmologists Buddhists are now undertaking.

The Challenge to Buddhist Tradition

For the most part, Buddhists have, to this date, stressed environmental ethics and psychology in their conversations with the natural sciences.[19] This assertion does not imply that Buddhists have paid no attention to physics and biology. But, as in Christian theology, the focus of Buddhist interest in the natural sciences has stressed those areas where traditional Buddhist teachings might be supported by current scientific views of physical reality.

In general, Buddhists interpret all of the natural sciences as a support for their doctrine of interdependence (*pratītya-samutpāda*, or "dependent co-origination"), which teaches that every thing and event at every moment of space-time is cocreated and constituted by the interdependently interpenetrating nexus of relationships it undergoes from moment to moment of its existence. In point of fact, Buddhist understanding of interdependence and scientific descriptions of the interdependence of physical relationships, in both physics and biology, are remarkably congruent. Thus, Buddhist interest in ecology is closely linked to the Buddhist doctrine of dependent co-origination, as are Buddhist teachings about nonself (*anatta, anātman*). Furthermore, the centrality of the practice of meditation has led Buddhists to the various disciplines comprising the neurosciences and a means of translating its traditional doctrines of suffering and its causes (*duḥkha* and *taṇhā*), the meaning of Awakening (*nirvāṇa*), and the discipline of meditation into more contemporary contexts, which will be described in chapter 5.

B. Alan Wallace, who writes about the relation between scientific theory and reality through the lenses of his Tibetan Buddhist lineage, will serve to illustrate both a Buddhist critique of physics and biology and a Buddhist interest in psychology and the neurosciences. In contrast to Barbour, Wallace is highly critical of the principle of "critical realism" in that he thinks that no scientific theory has "ontological correspondence to physical realities."[20] Neither Barbour's "independence model" nor Cabezón's "conflict/ambivalence model" describes Wallace's thesis about the relation between science and Buddhism. According to Wallace, "while the sciences give us objective knowledge about physical processes, the sciences do not give us knowledge of an objective world."[21] This means that the function of any scientific theory is to make natural events intelligible for the purpose of developing technology that improves the quality of life for "all sentient beings." In other words, Wallace takes an instrumentalist approach to scientific inquiry that views scientific truth as pragmatic, meaning truths leading to practical technological applications that improve the quality of life for all sentient beings.

Wallace's interpretation of the natural sciences is based on his appropriation of the "two-truth" epistemology that originated with the second-century Indian Buddhist logician Nagarjuna.[22] As pragmatic truths about the physical world, scientific truths are "secondary truths" that in themselves shed no light on the nature of reality. Absolute truth, however, is metaphysical and is named by Wallace, following Nagarjuna, "Emptying" (śūnyatā). "Emptying" is the absolute truth to which Buddhas awaken through the practice of meditation. Therefore, Wallace concludes, "we err if we expect the natural sciences to solve issues of a metaphysical or religious nature, for they were never designed to probe such questions."[23] Furthermore, as "secondary truths," the primary weakness of physics and the biological sciences is that "neither discipline[s] the mind and mental experience,"[24] a conclusion the majority of working scientists would not accept.

Geoffrey Redmond notes that Buddhism first encountered Western science as part of its experiences of eighteenth-century colonialism in South and East Asia. In this encounter, Buddhists do not appear to have felt the need to oppose Western science. Nor did the sciences challenge the fundamentals of Buddhism's worldview and doctrines in the way it challenged Christian theology. According to Redmond, this is because Buddhism is not committed to the prescientific ideas associated with it since Buddhism's traditional cosmology was never its essential core. Therefore, Buddhism was, and still is, less threatened by science than other world religions.[25] Like Wallace, Redmond thinks Buddhism and the sciences are independent enterprises.

Victor Mansfield takes Redmond's conclusions farther because he views the relation between the sciences and Buddhism through what Cabezón describes as the "complementarity model." Mansfield argues that similarities between Madhyamika philosophy and modern physics in their understanding of time are evidence that Buddhism is particularly compatible with the natural sciences, especially in the area of psychology.[26] But compatibility with the natural sciences does not imply that Buddhism is "scientific." Both Redmond and Mansfield, as well as most Buddhists, think that asserting that Buddhism is "scientific" is a distortion of both Buddhism and science. So, while science is no threat to Buddhist teachings and practice (because they are compatible enterprises), Buddhism has resources that can fill in the "gaps" of Western science relative to analyzing subjective mental and emotional experiences that can help the psychological sciences overcome the current Cartesian emphasis on objectivity and mind-body dualism and thereby develop more coherent theories of cognition.[27] In other words, through dialogue with Buddhism, science is more apt to be creatively transformed than is Buddhism because of Buddhism's "strong empirical foundations" and the "deconstructive traditions of Nagarjuna's Madhyamika ("middle way") dialectics," which Mansfield believes overcomes the "objectivist weakness" he perceives in Western physics and biology.[28]

Finally, writing from a Theravada Buddhist perspective, Shoyo Taniguchi is one of the few Buddhists who assert that Buddhism is "scientific." She scrutinizes the Pali *suttas* (*sutra* in Sanskrit, meaning "discourse of the Buddha") and early Buddhist philosophy and pushes Cabezón's "complementarity/ identity model" as far as it can probably be pushed. She concludes that early Theravada Buddhism employs empirical and experimental methods equivalent to those of modern science and is therefore a "scientific religion," meaning that Buddhist doctrines harmonize with current scientific models of physical reality in a way other religions do not.[29] Her explicit conclusion is that "Buddhism is thereby superior to other religions," particularly Judaism, Christianity, and Islam. In her view, physics and evolutionary biology leave no room for a creator.

It is clear that neither Wallace, Redmond, Mansfield, nor Taniguchi experiences or interprets the natural sciences, particularly Big Bang cosmology, as a challenge to Buddhist doctrine and practice. The distinct impression that contemporary Buddhist writing on the natural sciences seems to give is that the structure of Buddhist tradition remains untouched by all of the natural sciences, either positively or negatively.

Concluding Observations

It's now time to bring this chapter to a conclusion by considering what, if anything, Buddhist-Christian dialogue with the natural sciences would add to a current Buddhist-Christian encounter. First, it is clear that Buddhists

tend to read Big Bang cosmology, as well as evolutionary theory, as supportive of the Buddhist worldview. Buddhists seem not to have experienced the
natural sciences as a conceptual challenge to the same degree as Christians.
Some Buddhist writers point to parallels between Buddhism's "nontheistic"
worldview and current scientific cosmology as evidence that Buddhism
is more in harmony with the sciences than Christian theism (Wallace,
Redmond, and Mansfield). A few Buddhist writers, like Taniguchi, take a
stronger stance and affirm that scientific accounts of reality are proof of the
superiority of Buddhism to all theistic religions.

Such arguments have a familiar ring. Nineteenth- and early-twentieth-
century Western scholarly interpretations of Buddhism tended to see Buddhism as "rational," "experimental," "empirical," and, thereby, "critical of
authority" beyond an individual's own experience—all treasured philosophical ideals of the Western Enlightenment. And, indeed, Buddhists
have generally not thought it necessary to rethink or reformulate the fundamental doctrines that shape Buddhist thought and practice because of
challenges posed by its encounter with the natural sciences. So, it seems, at
first glance, that Buddhists have concluded that conceptual dialogue with
the natural sciences as a "third party" would contribute as little to Buddhism's creative transformation.

However, Buddhists are as interested in the natural sciences as Christians,
particularly in the practice of "socially engaged dialogue" with Christian traditions of social activism. Buddhists have learned much from Christian tradition about confronting issues of oppression and injustice that are not religion specific: consumerism, gender issues, social justice issues, environmental
issues, racism, war. The biological sciences have been particularly helpful to
Buddhists and Christians in their socially engaged dialogue on environmental issues because these problems cannot be addressed apart from what evolutionary biology tells us about the structures of organic processes. Therefore,
a point of entry for Buddhist-Christian dialogue with the natural sciences
might well be socially engaged dialogue. Including the sciences as a third
partner in socially engaged dialogue, especially the biological sciences and
economics, would greatly empower current Buddhist and Christian cooperation in confronting justice and environmental issues.

Finally, the neurobiological sciences might also make important contributions to the practice of Buddhist-Christian interior dialogue, given the psychological and neurological processes underlying practices like mediation in
Buddhism and contemplative prayer in Christian tradition. The specifics of
Buddhist interest in the neurosciences will be discussed in chapter 5. For
now, it will suffice to note that the psychological dynamics and neurophysi-

ological processes underlying Buddhist meditative practice and Christian prayer practices might shed new light on Buddhist and Christian religious experience, in terms of both similarities and differences between the experiences such practices engender. Furthermore, such scientific research might also shed light on the nature of religious experience as such. Accordingly, new information might be added to what is already known about Buddhist and Christian practice traditions.

Notes

1. This chapter includes material already published in a previous essay titled "A Reflection on Buddhist-Christian Dialogue with the Natural Sciences," in *Fifty Years in Science and Religion: Ian G. Barbour and His Legacy*, ed. Robert John Russell (Burlington, VT: Ashgate Publishing, 2004), 315–28.

2. John Polkinghorne, *Belief in God in an Age of Science* (New Haven, CT: Yale University Press, 1998), xiii.

3. See Jonathan J. Halliwell, "Quantum Cosmology and the Creation of the Universe," in *Cosmology: Historical, Literary, Philosophical, Religious, and Scientific Perspectives* (New York: Garland Publishing, 1993), 477–97.

4. See Steven Weinberg, *The First Three Minutes* (New York: Basic Books, 1988).

5. Alan Guth and Paul Steinhard, "The Inflationary Universe," *Scientific American* 250 (May 1984): 116–28.

6. Stephen W. Hawking, *A Brief History of Time* (New York: Bantam Books, 1988), 141. Hawking makes similar observations about God in his revision of this book titled *A Briefer History of Time* (New York: Bantam, 2005), 137–42.

7. Geoffrey P. Redmond, "Comparing Science and Buddhism," *The Pacific World* 11–12 (1995–1996): 106.

8. Redmond, "Comparing Science and Buddhism," 111.

9. *De civitate dei* (*The City of God*), XII, 15, cited in Russell Stannard, "Where in the World Is God?" *Research News and Opportunities in Science and Theology* 1 (October 2000): 13.

10. See Etienne Gilson, *The Christian Philosophy of Saint Augustine* (New York: Random House, 1960), 190–91.

11. Augustine, *Confessiones*, book 11, in *Confessions* (Oxford: Oxford University Press, 1991), 230.

12. *De civitate dei*, XII, 15: "For where there is no creature whose changing movements admits to succession, there cannot be time at all." See also XI, 6: "time does not exist without some movement and transition." Also see Robert Jordan, "Time and Contingency in St. Augustine," in *Augustine: A Collection of Critical Essays*, ed. R. A. Markus (New York: Anchor Books, 1972), 255–79, and Hugh Lacy, "Empiricism and Augustine's Problem about Time," in Markus, *Augustine*, 280–308.

13. Langdon Gilkey, *Maker of Heaven and Earth: The Christian Doctrine of Creation in Light of Modern Knowledge* (Garden City, NY: Doubleday, 1959), 310–15.

14. Ian G. Barbour, *Religion and Science: Historical and Contemporary Issues* (San Francisco: Harper San Francisco, 1997), 128–29.

15. Barbour, *Religion and Science*, 129.

16. Robert John Russell, "Finite Creation without a Beginning," in *Quantum Cosmology and the Laws of Nature: Scientific Perspectives on Divine Action*, ed. Robert John Russell, Nancy Murphy, and C. J. Isham (Vatican City: Vatican Observatory and the Center for Theology and the Natural Sciences, 1996), 302.

17. See Shoyo Taniguchi, "Modern Science and Early Buddhist Ethics: Methodology of Two Disciplines," *The Pacific World* 11–12 (1995–1996): 45–53.

18. Paul Tillich, *Systematic Theology I* (Chicago: University of Chicago Press, 1951), 235–92.

19. See, for example, Mary Evelyn Tucker and Duncan Ryukan Williams, eds., *Buddhism and Ecology* (Cambridge, MA: Harvard University Press, 1997), and three essays in J. Baird Callicott and Roger T. Ames, eds., *Nature in Asian Traditions of Thought* (Albany: State University of New York, 1989): Francis Cook, "The Jeweled Net of Indra" (213–30), Kenneth K. Inada "Environmental Problems" (231–46), and David J. Kaluphana, "Toward a Middle Path of Survival" (247–58).

20. B. Alan Wallace, *Choosing Reality: A Buddhist View of Physics and Mind* (Ithaca, NY: Snow Lion Press, 1996), ch. 11.

21. Wallace, *Choosing Reality*, 14.

22. For an interpretation and translation of Nagarjuna's writings, see Frederick J. Streng, *Emptiness: A Study in Religious Meaning* (Nashville: Abingdon Press, 1967).

23. Streng, *Emptiness*, 9.

24. Streng, *Emptiness*, 9.

25. Geoffrey Redmond, "Introduction," *The Pacific World* 11–12 (1995–1996): 2–3. Also see "Comparing Science and Buddhism," *The Pacific World* 11–12 (1995–1996): 101–14.

26. Victor Mansfield, "Time in Madhyamika Buddhism and Modern Physics," *The Pacific World* 11–12 (1995–1996): 28–67.

27. This will be described more fully in chapter 5.

28. Mansfield, "Time in Madhyamika Buddhism and Modern Physics," 65–67.

29. Taniguchi, "Modern Science and Early Buddhist Ethics," 45–53.

~

CHAPTER FOUR

Christian and Buddhist Responses to Evolutionary Biology

A rather priggish version of the history of ideas held by a number of physicists, biologists, and historians of science asserts that there is a parallel between Copernicus's displacement of the Earth as the center of the universe and Charles Darwin's theoretical explanation of the origins of species through natural selection operating through chance and necessity over great lengths of time. According to this theory, the Copernican revolution displaced the Earth from its previously accepted location as the center of the universe—as Aristotle's philosophy was read through the filter of the Genesis creation story until the sixteenth century—and Earth became one more planet revolving around the sun.[1] In a similar way, the Darwinian revolution displaced human beings from their position at the center of life on Earth with all other species being created by God to serve human interests. After Darwin, the human species became one among many on a living planet, so that human beings are the relatives of chimpanzees, gorillas, and, in fact, all life-forms by a common ancestry. In both revolutions, God as an explanatory category for scientific processes became irrelevant.

While this interpretation of the two revolutions in science is true, it is inadequate because it leaves out what is most important: they are the beginning of "science" in the modern sense of the word and, therefore, can be seen together as the beginning of one scientific revolution that is still, in many ways, an ongoing process with two interdependent stages, the Copernican and the Darwinian. This chapter focuses on the Darwinian part of the scientific revolution and its implications for Buddhist-Christian dialogue.

According to Francisco J. Ayala, Darwin completed the Copernican revolution's central notion that nature is a lawful system of matter in motion.[2] The adaptations and diversity of living organisms, the origin of novel and highly organized forms of living organisms, the origin of the human species itself, could be explained as an orderly process of change governed by natural laws organizing matter in motion without reference to religious myths or God.

But Darwin faced a real problem when he wrote *Origin of Species*. A version of the argument by design was almost universally held among intellectuals of his day, including both theologians and naturalists. The most popular version of this argument was English clergyman William Paley's *Natural Theology*. Indeed, Darwin himself read *Natural Theology* as a university student and found it much to his liking, but later changed his mind. Paley possessed extensive and accurate biological knowledge, as detailed and precise as possible in the 1800s. His book is a sustained "argument by design" that claims that the living world provides compelling evidence of being designed by an omniscient and omnipotent creator. The core of Paley's argument is his claim that "[t]here cannot be design without a designer; contrivance, without a contriver; order, without choice; . . . means suitable to an end, and executing their office in accomplishing that end, without the end ever having been contemplated."[3] Again and again, Paley draws the conclusion that only an omniscient and omnipotent deity could account for the complexity and order of the structure of biological processes. Thus, as a person finding a watch on a beach can draw the certain conclusion that a watchmaker exists, so the structure of the human eye can only be explained by the existence of a deity who designed it.

Darwin accepted the idea that organisms are "designed," but not by a creator. He argued that inherited adaptive variations, adaptations useful in the survival of species in their particular environments, are most likely to appear in organisms. When these adaptive variations occur, the odds for an organism's survival are increased over those of organisms in the same species that do not have these adaptations. Those who do survive pass on their adaptive variations to future generations because they are most successful in reproduction, while those members of a species that have not adapted die off. Darwin's term for the preservation of favorable variations and the rejection of unfavorable variations is *natural selection*. If enough favorable adaptations are passed reproductively to new generations over time, the original species will become extinct and be replaced by a new species suitable for survival in its environment. In this way, evolution is a process of natural selection that "designs" all organisms.

Exactly how natural selection occurs is not clear in Darwin's original theory of evolution. It was the rediscovery in 1900 of Gregor Mendel's theory of hereditary that brought genetics into evolutionary theory as a means of explaining how natural selection actually takes place. Accordingly, contemporary interpretations of natural selection are formulated in genetic and statistical terms as differential reproduction, a form of evolutionary theory often referred to as "neo-Darwinism" by nonscientists, although this term is little used by most working scientists. According to contemporary interpretations, natural selection causes some genes and genetic combinations to have higher probabilities of being transmitted than their alternatives. These genetic units will become more common in subsequent generations, and their alternatives, less common. In other words, natural selection over time is a statistical bias in the relative rate of reproduction of alternative genes. In this way, natural selection acts like a filtering sieve by eliminating harmful genetic variations and retaining beneficial ones. But natural selection is also much more than a purely negative process because it is able to generate novelty by increasing the probability of otherwise extremely improbable genetic combinations. In this way, natural selection is a creative process in the sense that, while it does not "create" the entities upon which it operates, it produces adaptive and functional genetic combinations in living organisms that could not have existed otherwise.

Natural selection has no foresight; nor does it operate according to some preconceived plan. It is strictly nonpersonal, a purely natural process resulting from the interaction of the properties of physicochemical and biological entities. It does have the appearance of purposefulness because it is conditioned by environmental factors: which organisms reproduce more effectively depends on which variations they possess that are useful in the place and time where organisms live. While natural selection does not "anticipate" the environments of living organisms, however, drastic environmental changes may be too quick for organisms to adapt to. Species extinction is a common outcome of evolutionary processes, and more than 99 percent of all species that have ever lived on the Earth have become extinct. Consequently, natural selection does not strive to produce predetermined kinds of organisms but only organisms that are adapted to their particular environments.

The exact nature of the role chance and necessity, or in more philosophical language, contingency and determinism, in natural selection is a hotly debated topic among scientists and Christian theologians in dialogue with the natural sciences. According to standard interpretations in biology, natural selection accounts for the "design" of organisms because variations tend to increase the probability of their carriers' survival and reproduction at the expense of less adaptive variations. From simple bacteria to human beings, the traits that organisms acquire in their evolutionary histories are not fortuitous but determined by their functional utility for the organisms, "designed," as it were, to serve their life needs in particular environments. The force that drives the "design" of natural selection is the genetic mutation of genes passed on reproductively over time.

However, according to George V. Coyne, the problem of the relation between chance and necessity is not formulated correctly by most biologists and philosophers of science. He writes,

> It is not just a question of chance or necessity because, first of all, it is both. Furthermore, there is a third element here that is very important. It is what might be called "opportunity," and it is based upon our scientific knowledge of the universe. The universe is so prolific in offering opportunity for the success of both chance and necessary processes that such a character of the universe must be included in the discussion.[4]

That is, mutation cannot, by itself, account for adaptation or design. Mutations occur in single individuals, and even if a mutation occurs repeatedly in a species consisting of many individuals, it will never extend to all members of the species because particular mutations will be, over time, counteracted by other mutations and, thereby, disappear. Natural selection can accomplish adaptation because a favorable mutation that has occurred in one individual may spread to the whole species in a few generations, and with a high probability on the scale of the low probability of mutations.

Nevertheless, chance remains an integral part of the process of evolution. Mutations that yield the hereditary variations available to natural selection arise at random, independently of whether they are beneficial or harmful to their carriers. This random process is counteracted by natural selection, which preserves what is useful for survival as it eliminates what is harmful for survival. Without mutations, evolution could not happen because there would be no variations to convey from one generation to another. But again, without natural selection, the mutation process would yield disorganization and extinction because mutations are disadvantageous and occur erratically. Mutation and natural selection have jointly driven the process of evolution that has "created" all life, from microscopic organisms, to the Douglas firs that surround my home on Puget Sound, to the bald eagles that occasionally nest in these trees, to human beings. Furthermore, these same processes have generated life wherever it may occur in the universe.

The theory of evolution thus portrays chance, necessity, and "opportunity" as jointly interdependent, as contingency and determinism jointly interlocked in the environmental "opportunity" inherent in natural processes from which have emerged the most complex, diverse, and beautiful entities in the universe. This was Darwin's fundamental discovery that completes the scientific revolution initiated by Copernicus: everything in nature, including the "design" of living organisms, can be accounted for as the result of natural processes governed by natural laws without reference to God as a designer. In addition, the evidence supporting evolution is overwhelming and has been obtained by paleontology, comparative anatomy, biogeography, embryology, biochemistry, molecular genetics, and other biological disciplines. This is why the role of chance and necessity in natural selection, as one of the most solid conclusions of contemporary science, poses serious challenges to monotheistic traditions like Christianity, Judaism, and Islam. All living organisms, past, present, and future, come to be as a result of the interplay of chance and necessity over time.[5]

Even so, there is much that biologists do not understand. Precisely how do human beings come to be in this immensely changing and interdependent universe of galaxies and stars? It is very clear that biologists do not know everything about this process; nor do many biologists claim such knowledge. But from an evolutionary standpoint, it is absurd to deny, for example, that the human brain is the end result of physical processes of chemical complexity in an evolving universe. After the universe became rich in certain basic chemicals, these chemicals combined in successive steps to make ever more complex molecules. Finally, in another series of extraordinary chemical processes, the human brain, the most complicated biological structure that we know, came to be.

What degree of certainty can be placed in this current evolutionary picture? It is certainly true that biologists do not have enough knowledge to say how every living organism came to be. No one knows precisely how each complex chemical system brought about the diversity of life-forms that currently inhabit the planet Earth—or any other place where life might occur in the universe. Finally, scientists are at present ignorant about the elements in nature from which have emerged the unbroken genealogical continuity in evolution that biologists propose actually happened and is still happening. There exists, in other words, a number of epistemological gaps that prevent biologists from concluding that a detailed theory of evolution has been proven with absolute certainty. It is certain that the theory of evolution provides the most adequate account now conceivable concerning the available empirical biological and physical data. This fact creates an opening for interreligious dialogue with evolutionary biology, even as it presents serious challenges to all religious worldviews.

Christian Responses to Evolutionary Biology

The challenge evolution poses to Christian faith and practice is threefold. First, evolutionary theory asserts that variations leading to the origin and differentiation of species are random, in the sense of being "undirected." The apparent absence of intelligent control over the contingencies of evolution suggests that novelty in nature is thoroughly "accidental," so that there is no necessity for divine influence governing the world. Today, the sources of life's variations have been identified as genetic mutation, and most biologists follow Darwin in attributing the variations to "chance." Second, the fact that individual organisms must struggle for survival, as well as that the vast majority suffer and lose out in this struggle, points to the underlying indifference of natural selection, the mechanism that ruthlessly eliminates weaker organisms. Finally, life's experiments have required an almost unimaginable amount of time for the diversity of species to come about. The fact that evolution requires many billions of years to bring about intelligent beings capable of understanding this process seems to be clear evidence that neither life nor mind is the result of an intelligent divine plan for the universe.

Before Darwin published *Origin of Species*, the notion of special creation, or the view that God created the universe and all contained therein for God's special purposes, dominated Western thought generally and Christian theology particularly. For centuries mainstream science—"natural history," as it was then called—supported this view of origins. Species are "fixed" and breed true to form; they do not evolve. So, as European natural historians came to appreciate the complex balances ingredient in nature, many came to believe that this was evidence for the existence of a creator god. Particularly in the Protestant countries of Britain and northern Europe, where the natural sciences gained a certain cultural authority during the seventeenth and eighteenth centuries, natural history became the handmaid of natural theology, as classically expressed in William Paley's *Natural Theology*.

Most nineteenth-century biologists accepted Darwin's theory, although some, like the American biologist Louis Agassiz, challenged Darwin's theory by arguing that highly complex individual organs (like the human eye) and ecologically sensitive species (such as bees and flowers) cannot evolve through the sort of minute, random steps envisioned by Darwin. To survive, Agassiz argued, each modification must be beneficial. But complex organs and organic relationships only work as a whole. They cannot develop in steps. So, he proposed that complex organisms reflect intelligent design and, thus, testify to both the existence and creativity of God as designer.[6]

The early religious opposition to Darwin relied heavily on scientific views such as Agassiz's and is still playing itself out in the twenty-first century, especially among Christian fundamentalists and some Protestant evangelicals, particularly in the United States. Specifically, two forms of Christian opposition to evolutionary theory today are examples of Ian Barbour's conflict model. First, evolutionary biology is in conflict with literalist readings of the Bible, most notably the Genesis creation stories in chapters 1 and 2, which declare that God created the Earth and all of its species in six days. Accepting the Genesis creation stories as literal fact is the foundation of fundamentalist Christian assertions of special creationism in biology, as well as their rejection of contemporary scientific evidence supporting evolution, particularly the geological evidence that Earth has been changing and evolving for four billion years.

Second, many evangelical Christians who accept the theory of evolution are deeply troubled by the broader theological implications regarding the experience of suffering. What sort of God would create living species through random chance mutations and a painful struggle for existence? Can such a god be called "good" and omnipotent? Thus, since God could use evolutionary processes operating over eons of time to create the diversity of life, evangelical Christians think that the total exclusion of God from any role in the origin and preservation of life is both presumptuous and preposterous. While most evangelical Christians are not creationists, most evangelical theologians, the classic example being Karl Barth, understand evolutionary theory and Christian faith and practice as independent enterprises. However, there are important neo-orthodox theologians who are very open to the natural sciences in general and evolutionary theory in particular, perhaps the most notable being Langdon Gilkey.

Gilkey fully accepts evolutionary theory and concludes that Christian faith and practice should be contextualized by evolutionary descriptions of biological processes. But such acceptance should not be uncritical. He observes that natural selection cannot, as an explanatory biological principle, provide the causes for the changes and forms of life or for the overall story of life because (1) a chance event in nature is an unexplained event, so (2) using words like "chance" and "random" to explain evolutionary process makes biological explanations of these events impossible. He writes,

> In discussions of human beings and of all their works . . . the historical influences of *nature* must be set down with the historical influence of *cultural*

traditions (nature, culture, and community) and the influence of immediate *social environment* (family and community), that is "nurture," as providing the (creaturely or natural) explanatory factors of what we are and do. All our possibilities, or what we are and what we do alike, are genetic; our physical, psychological, moral, and spiritual similarities, as well as our differences, are patterned here. Thus, it is true that our social customs, manners, laws, obligations (morals), as well as our religious rites, myths, and laws, can be traced back—as can our bones and our organs—into the dim recesses of the prehuman past. And biology, medicine, and genetics, in fact, the entire corpus of science, can likewise be traced back to those origins.[7]

In other words, speaking theologically, evolution is the way God creates: in and through the "providential story of cosmic and evolutionary development."[8]

The best-known examples of contemporary creationist movements are "scientific creationism" and its more sophisticated offspring, "intelligent design." Since both assume a basic conflict between all scientific conclusions and theories that contradict literalist readings of Genesis and other parts of the Bible, theological dialogue with the natural sciences is in principle impossible. The term *scientific creationism* originated with Henry Morris, who taught engineering at the Virginia Polytechnic Institute. The publication of his book, *The Genesis Flood*, in 1961 gave biblical literalists scientific-sounding support for the biblical account of a six-day creation six thousand years ago. It was this book that created the "creation science" movement within American fundamentalism with Morris as its primary spokesperson. Morris still leads this movement through the Institute for Creation Research, which is headquartered in Seattle, Washington.

The intelligent design movement is a contemporary version of the pre-Darwinian era of natural history. The best-known authority in the intelligent movement is Michael Behe, who teaches biochemistry at Lehigh University.[9] Behe, a devout Roman Catholic, challenges all evolutionary explanations for complex organic processes by reviving pre-Darwinian arguments from design based on evidence of nature's complexity. In fact, Behe's published work seems like a contemporary rereading of William Paley's *Natural Theology*, with Paley's eighteenth-century English prose replaced by Behe's twenty-first-century prose, plus his considerable knowledge of contemporary science.

Unlike creationists like Morris, Behe does not argue for a "young Earth" but proposes that intelligent design, rather than random chance, is empirically evident in natural processes. In this way, Behe divorces intelligent design from creation science and argues that intelligent design should be taught in biology courses in public schools, along with, and as an alternative to, standard evolutionary theory. In its basic approach, therefore, intelligent design is much older than creation science. Yet, like Protestant fundamentalism, creation science has had a rather short history. Both movements reach out beyond Protestant fundamentalism to conservative evangelicals and Roman Catholics. Both movements reject the methodological naturalism of scientific method and object to teaching the conclusions of evolutionary theory as fact in the public schools. Although the intelligent design movement has not as yet gained the mass following of scientific creationism, its followers now play a pivotal role in the controversy, mostly in the United States, surrounding the teaching of evolution.[10]

One would expect that the scientific community would find the intelligent design movement's claim to being "scientific" indefensible. But many theologians active in the science-religion dialogue are also quite critical of the intelligent design movement. One of the most succinct criticisms is that of physicist-theologian Robert John Russell, founder of the Center for Theology and the Natural Sciences in Berkeley, California. Since supporters of intelligent design do not specify what they mean by the intelligent agency that supposedly accounts for the origin and evolution of life, there are only two options for what "agency" can mean: either a natural agent or God. The first option ultimately relies on the very theory that intelligent design rejects, Darwinian evolution, and the second is a theological claim. The second claim, that God is the intelligent agent at work in the origins of life, is certainly a defensible option, but not as a scientific claim. It is a theological claim resting upon much wider bodies of experience than that investigated by science. Therefore, Russell concludes, intelligent design should not be taught in public school science classes because, given the nature and object of scientific inquiry, issues of divine agency can never be an object of scientific investigation.[11]

Restated somewhat differently, because "seeing the world as it physically is" is the business of science (but not only science), scientific *method* requires scientists to investigate honestly and let the chips fall where they may. For this reason alone, it is inconceivable that religious texts or specific doctrines can add anything to scientific *method* or scientific conclusions. The intelligent design movement is rightly seen as misguided insofar as it purports to put, because of certain theological presuppositions, the outcome ahead of the exploration. The intelligent design movement has lifted off from scientific practice into the realm of theological speculation, that is, has confused science with theology, and it is a mistake to confuse intelligent design with the pursuit of science.

However, many theologians who reject the conclusions of the intelligent design movement seek to deepen the relevance of contemporary Christian faith and practice through dialogue with the evolutionary sciences. While there exists great diversity of opinion among these writers, they are united by several common assumptions. First, scientific conclusions regarding natural processes are factual descriptions corresponding to physical reality but capable of revision. Most are critical realists. Second, all take the Bible seriously but never literally. This means that, for example, Adam and Eve are not historical figures, the Fall and the Flood are not historical events, the heavens and the Earth were not created in six days, and the sun did not stop its course when Joshua attacked the city of Jericho. Because these events are physically impossible, these stores must be interpreted symbolically to discern their proper theological meanings. Third, all affirm that Christian faith must be reconceived in relation to the realities of religious pluralism, as well as the natural sciences. Fourth, all are open to the practice of interreligious dialogue and dialogue with the natural sciences as a means of creatively transforming Christian faith and practice.

Permeating all science-theology dialogue is the question of divine action, which may in fact represent evolution's single greatest challenge to Christian (and Jewish and Muslim) theology. Given the number of theologians who have given attention to this issue, is not possible to give a complete account here of all the important writers in this area. Consequently, I shall focus on the views of two theologians, Arthur Peacocke and John Haught, as a means of illustrating some of the essential themes of Christian theological reflection on contemporary evolutionary biology.

Arthur Peacocke, a biologist-theologian who worked in the field of biochemistry at the Universities of Birmingham and Oxford, has argued that the assumption that the relation between science and religion is best described as a "state of war" is historically inaccurate.[12] According to Peacocke, the relation between science and religion has always been "symbiotic" because both are involved in the human quest for intelligibility and meaning. Given this, all faith communities, particularly Christian faith communities, should reflect more profoundly on the experience of nature as described in the natural sciences.[13] He writes,

> For, in spite of the corrosion . . . of post-modernist relativities, scientists and religious believers share a common conviction that they are dealing with reality in their respective enterprises. Scientists would give up if they ceased to see themselves as discovering the structures and processes of nature, even if only approximately—and the exercise of worship, meditation, and prayer

would be vacuous if the Ultimate Reality . . . to whom they were directed were not regarded as real.[14]

So, both science and theology seek to understand reality, which is not to say that either is always successful. This implies that there exists some common ground for theologians and scientists to engage in dialogue. Although one can neither prove nor disprove the existence of God or the specific claims of Christian faith and practice about the historical Jesus by means of scientific conclusions about natural processes—the error of natural theology traditions based on design arguments such as Paley's—a Christian who takes the sciences seriously may reasonably believe in the existence of God as an "inference to the best explanation." This is so because the sciences enforce the long-held intuition of theists that God is (1) one; (2) the underlying "ground of being" of all that exists, past, present, and future; and (3) the source of the deep unity, interconnectedness, and wholeness of existence.

According to Peacocke, scientific descriptions of nature, particularly evolutionary theory (and physics), allow Christians to affirm reasonably that there must exist a God who is (1) one and experiences unfathomable richness of experience; (2) supremely rational; (3) a sustainer and faithful preserver; (4) a continual creator of an "anthropic universe"; (5) purposeful; (6) always in process of becoming; (7) able to experience joy and delight in creation; (8) the source of the interplay of indeterminacy and law; (9) "self-limited omnipotent and omniscient"; (10) vulnerable, self-emptying, and self-giving love; and (11) suffering because God experiences the suffering of all sentient beings, just as God experiences the joys of all sentient beings.[15]

So, the question is, how, given the role of natural selection operating through chance and necessity over time contextualized by environmental factors, is divine action in the universe possible? Simply identifying God with the universe is problematic because theism requires that God is, in some sense, the creator of the universe. Pantheism is not a viable theological option. But if God's actions come from outside the universe, they will conflict with natural laws and introduce new energies into closed physical systems, which will set theological reflection in conflict with science. But if God is conceived of as somehow immanent within with the universe, divine action can be understood as supplemental to physical events, utilizing their energies and physical structures.

In reflecting on this issue, Peacocke notes that the sort of causality that most often has been understood by scientists to operate in nature is "bottom-up causality"; that is, the properties of a whole system, for example a cell, is the result of the interactions of the molecules, atoms, and quarks that comprise the cell. So, the behavior of the whole (the cell) is deter-mined by its constituent "lower-level" units; that is, the whole (the cell) and its functions are determined by the causal behavior of its constituent parts (the cell's quarks, atoms, and molecules).

However, chaos theory, systems theory, and thermodynamics have over the past fifty years revealed the role of top-down causation at work in many phys-ical systems. For example, according to the Second Law of Thermodynamics, in isolated systems undergoing irreversible processes far from equilibrium, the entropy, or disorder, within such systems always increases. This is why no sys-tem, including the universe or life-forms in the universe, is permanent. But there also emerge new more ordered, or "organized," systems from systems un-dergoing entropy. This means that in far-from-equilibrium, nonlinear, open systems, matter displays a potential to be self-organizing and capable of bring-ing into existence new forms by the operation of internal forces and proper-ties, now operating under the constraints afforded by their being incorporated into systems whose properties, as a whole, now have to be taken into account. In other words, changes at lower microscopic levels of a physical system oc-cur because of top-down casual influences (e.g., the molecules of a cell are what they are *because* of their incorporation into the system as a whole, that is, the cell, the organ of which the cell is a part, and ultimately the entire body of a living organism). In other words, the whole (the cell) "constrains," or sets the "boundary conditions" of, the causal actions of its constituent parts (the cell's quarks, atoms, and molecules). So, the whole cannot be reduced to, or entirely explained by, its "lower-level" constituent parts.

This does not mean that the bottom-up explanation is of no scientific value. Peacocke's point is that both forms of causation are scientifically in-terdependent and that emphasizing either one while ignoring the other leads to the distortions of scientific reductionism.[16] Of course, theological language is always symbolic and analogical, especially in reference to God, but Pea-cocke appropriates the scientific fact of bottom-up and top-down causal in-terdependence as a metaphor through which to reflect on God's creation of the universe from the Big Bang singularity and God's subsequent interaction with the universe. Just as the human body is the boundary condition for the functioning of its individual cells constrained by environmental factors over time, one may think of the universe with all of its constituent parts as the "body" of God, which is Peacocke's way of thinking of God's immanence in the universe.[17] So, the universe is the kind of universe it is because of the way it is "constrained" by the exquisite balance between the four physical forces[18] holding it together, beginning at Plank time, in such a way that life on Earth began to evolve four billion years ago. The universe is "constrained" to be the kind of universe it is because God, as the boundary condition of the universe, is immanent "in, with, and under" all things and events at every moment of space-time—just as the evolution of the Earth's life-forms are constrained by the boundary conditions set by the particular physics of this universe in their individual environmental contexts.[19]

Peacocke's view of God is not pantheistic because, as a Christian, he thought God's nature, that is, God's eternal selfhood, which constitutes God as God, always transcends the universe, in much the same way that an artist expresses his or her creative selfhood in a painting, sculpture, or poem while remaining ontologically distinct from the work of art. In Peacocke's view, God's continuing action in the universe is like the creative act of an artist, the difference being that an artist completes a work of art and moves on, while God remains continually creative in the processes of the universe everywhere these processes occur. This includes the processes of evolution.

Of course, all Christian theologians believe that God created the universe and is continually active in guiding the course of the universe's history. But there is a good deal of debate about how, given the laws of science, divine action is possible. Specifically, Peacocke draws on the experimental evidence of biology by appropriating the notion of "emergence" as a means of conceiving divine action. In the natural sciences, emergence is the view that new and unpredictable phenomena are naturally produced by interactions in nature; that these new structures and organisms are not reducible to the subsystems on which they depend; and that the newly evolved realities in turn exercise causal influence on the parts out of which they arise. Indeed, one of the facts established by both physics and evolutionary biology is that, at increasing levels of complexity, new properties emerge that are not predictable from the interactions of their lower levels of organization. For example, human consciousness, self-awareness, and mentality are not realities that can be adequately explained by the biochemical interactions of the molecules in the brain and central nervous system. None of the atoms and molecules of the human body "have" mental properties, so human consciousness, self-awareness, and mentality are emergent properties not reducible to the biochemical interactions of atoms and molecules. Of course, bottom-up interactions are necessary for consciousness, self-awareness, and mentality; apart from the biological foundations of the central nervous system and the brain, consciousness could not have emerged. But the emergence of consciousness is not reducible to the interactions of bottom-up physical interactions in the brain and central nervous system.[20]

In this sense, according to Peacocke, God engages in top-down, or "whole-part," interaction with the universe, so that divine action is indirect, occurring through a chain of levels acting in a "downward" way. In similarity to Christian process theology, this leads John Polkinghorne to a pantheistic understanding of God, meaning the view that God is "in, with, and under" all things and events in the universe at every moment of space-time, while simultaneously transcending the universe. Also, similar to process theologians, he rejects the historicity of the Fall as recorded in Genesis 2, as well as miracles, as events that contradict the laws of science. For him, the Fall is not a historical event, and "original sin" is a universal human failure to achieve one's fullest creative potential, with the exception of the historical Jesus, whom Peacocke regards as the "perfect human being" because of Jesus's complete replacement of his ego with his surrender to the will and purposes of God. Finally, Peacocke interprets God's top-down involvement with the universe to mean that God experiences the suffering of all life-forms necessitated by evolution as a creative means of drawing all life to future wholeness symbolized in the New Testament as the Kingdom of God.[21]

According to John Haught, the challenge of evolution to Christian faith lies in interpretations of scientific conclusions filtered through the screen of the reductionisms of philosophical materialism. "Furthermore," he writes, "if they looked closely at its contemporary scientific presentations, Jews, Muslims, Hindus, Buddhists, Jains, Taoists, primitive peoples and others as well, would see that evolution is a shock to their belief systems."[22] All religious traditions, not just Christian tradition, hold that there is some unfathomable "point," or purpose, to the universe and that the cosmos is enshrouded in meaning and purpose to which human beings ought to surrender. But given the long, hit-and-miss, and very often cruel way in which evolution appears to work, is it really feasible for any religious tradition to think of the universe as grounded in an ordering principle to which their ideas of a "sacred" reality are thought to point? Of course, Christians are in the same boat as other persons of faith in having to rethink questions of meaning and purpose. But is it feasible, Haught asks, that a process that impersonally "creates" the incredible complexities of Earth's life-forms through the random interplay of chance and necessity over time through natural selection, all without meaning or the need for a personally creating and sustaining designer, leaves any room for Christian faith in God? Yet, even as evolution constitutes the main challenge for contemporary Christian faith and practice, this very challenge also presents an opportunity for the creative transformation of Christian faith and practice. The reformulation of Christian theology in dialogue with evolutionary biology is what Haught calls "evolutionary theology," which involves six traditional themes reformulated in light of evolutionary science: (1) creation, (2) eschatology, (3) revelation, (4) grace, (5) divine power, and (6) redemption.

The notion that God created the universe is central to traditional Christian faith and practice. Traditionally, "creation" is understood as "original creation" (*creatio originalis*), "ongoing" or "continuing creation" (*creatio continua*), and "new creation" or the "fulfillment of creation" (*creatio nova*). Prior to the cosmological discoveries of physics, cosmology, and biological evolution, continuing creation and the fulfillment of creation were usually not given as much attention as original creation. Thus, creation meant that God did something "in the beginning," which, when pushed to extremes, leads to deism, or the view that God created the universe, then left it alone to run its course according to the natural laws God instituted "in the beginning." But the facts of evolution now allow theology to apprehend an ongoing and constantly new reality, which is not so easily apprehended through the lens of original creation. The Big Bang universe continues to unfold, and life continues to evolve wherever there is life, which means that the universe is always new. In a constantly changing universe, where life is continually evolving, every day is the dawn of a new creation. Thus, evolution allows theology to acknowledge that the notion of an originally instantaneous and created universe is scientifically and theologically incoherent. The universe remains unfinished. Moreover, the universe is an imperfect universe, where the appearance of evil and great suffering is demanded as the price of life itself. Evil and suffering represent the dark side of the universe's continuing creation. Indeed, no form of creation can occur without suffering. Due to this fact of existence, Christian faith looks toward the future eschatological completion of creation (*creatio nova*).[23]

In biblical tradition, eschatology is a type of theological reflection focused on what humanity might hope for as ultimate fulfillment. In an evolutionary context, however, humanity's hope for final fulfillment must be situated within the wider context of the ongoing creation of the entire universe.

> The epic of evolution invites us to extend our human hope outward and forward to embrace the entire cosmos, thus retrieving an often lost theme in the biblical wisdom literature and in the writings of St. Paul, St. Irenaeus, and many other religious thinkers who have also sought to bring the entire universe into the scheme of salvation.[24]

After Darwin, then, the universe can be apprehended as moving toward a future fulfillment that includes the entire sweep of evolution. Of course, this was also the point of Pierre Teilhard de Chardin, although Haught does not employ Teilhard's "Omega point" as a means of imagining the universe's final fulfillment.[25] Haught's point is that evolution fits quite well into the framework of biblical eschatology and, in doing so, gives eschatology a wider compass than the biblical writers could have ever imagined.

Haught asserts that evolution also helps theology to reformulate the idea of revelation. Revelation is not the communication of special prepositional information from a divine source of knowledge but the communication of God's own selfhood to persons. As such, revelation is the process whereby "the infinite" pours God's self fully and without reservation into creation everywhere creativity occurs. This revelatory outpouring is an expression of God's character as love. But the fullness of God's selfhood cannot be apprehended instantaneously by a finite cosmos. Such reception can only take place incrementally because a finite universe can only adapt itself to an infinite source of love by a gradual expansion and ongoing self-transcendence, the external manifestations of which might appear to science as cosmic and biological evolution.[26]

A theology of grace also makes intelligible the randomness, struggle, and natural selection that form the core of an evolutionary understanding of life. The doctrine of grace affirms that God loves the universe and all of its various elements and life-forms fully and unconditionally "with no strings attached." But, by definition, love does not absorb, annihilate, or force itself upon the beloved. Rather, love longs for the beloved to become more than the lover. Love longs for the beloved to become independent. Consequently, a central religious intuition of Christian faith is that God loves the universe and all things in it so that God's grace must mean "letting go" of the universe itself. In turn, this means that God's love refrains from forcing the divine presence on the universe or dissolving the universe into God. Only a relatively independent universe, a universe allowed to be itself, could be intimate with God. Theologically interpreted, then, evolution is a story of struggle toward an expansive freedom for all living things in the presence of God's self-giving grace. Seen from this point of view, randomness and the undirected features of evolution are essential features of any universe created by a gracious God.[27]

Of all the forms of contemporary theological reflection on the notion of divine power, process theology is the most attentive to evolutionary biology in the way in which it conceives how deeply God is involved with a universe wherein life on Earth meanders, experiments, strives, fails, and sometimes succeeds. In agreement with process theologians who draw upon the metaphysics of Alfred North Whitehead and Charles Hartshorne, Haught interprets biblical tradition about God's creative and redemptive power in ways that are fully consonant with the dynamic evolutionary character of life processes. In process theology, "divine power" means the "capacity to influence" so that "persuasive love," rather than coercion, is the defining character of divine power. God is therefore not a deity who magically forces things and events to fulfill divine intentions immediately in miraculous ways that contradict the laws of nature that God created. A coercive deity is one that immature religious minds often wish for and that scientific skeptics most often have in mind when they assert that evolutionary biology has destroyed theism. Thus, given the nature of God's character as love, God wills the independence of the universe, rather than being a despot who controls every event and wills every outcome.

A universe given the freedom to become more and more autonomous, even creating itself in the process and eventually attaining human consciousness and freedom, has much more integrity and value than any conceivable universe determined in every respect by a divine designer. Furthermore, divine power as coercive will is incompatible not only with human freedom but also with the prehuman spontaneity that allowed life to evolve into something other than its creator. So, evolution occurs, according to Haught, because a god of love is also the source of not only order but novelty. It is the introduction of novelty into the universe that makes evolution possible. God is more interested in the adventure of novelty than in preserving the status quo. In this sense, God's will is best understood as the maximization of cosmic beauty and intensity of experience for all living entities, so that "the epic of evolution is the world's response to God's own longing that it strive toward ever richer ways of realizing aesthetic intensity."[28] By offering new and rich possibilities to the universe, God sustains and creates the world continually. Or expressed in a more Whiteheadian way, God is more interested in "adventure than preserving the status quo."[29]

Again, drawing upon process philosophy, Haught believes that evolutionary biology can support a revised Christian understanding of redemption. The question is, given the perpetual perishing that is structurally part of all cosmic processes, for what can one reasonably hope? For Haught, the answer is the same as that given in biblical traditions and other monotheistic traditions, namely, that God is infinitely responsive to the universe and wherever life occurs in the universe. Because God's nature is love, the polar side of which is justice, like any lover, God "feels," or "prehends," the universe and all that occurs in the universe by taking it into God's self. God responds to the universe accordingly so that everything that occurs in the process of evolution is "saved" by being taken eternally into God's own feelings for the universe. As a consequence, even though all events and the achievements of evolution are impermanent, all things and events abide permanently within the everlasting compassion of God. As Haught summarizes this idea,

> In God's own sensitivity to the world, each event is redeemed from absolute perishing and receives the definitive importance and meaning that religions encourage us to believe—always without seeing clearly. That we abide in darkness on something of such ultimate moment is itself consistent with the fact that we live in an unfinished, imperfect universe; in other words, the only kind of universe consistent with the idea of an infinitely loving and active God.[30]

In reflecting on how God accomplishes the redemption of all living things that have evolved, are now evolving, or will evolve until the universe ends in a cold death trillions of years from now, Haught again draws upon Whitehead's metaphysics and current information theory. In this, his views are similar to John Polkinghorne's, although Polkinghorne's view is less indebted to Whitehead than Haught's. Since all life is embodied in physical processes, all life is embodied life. Thus, whatever hope can reasonably exist that death is not all there is lies in the resurrection of the body.

Neither Haught nor Polkinghorne mean by "resurrection" the resuscitation of our present physical structure. In Polkinghorne's "crude analogy,"

> The software running on our present hardware will be transformed to the hardware of the world to come. And where will that eschatological hardware come from? Surely the "matter" of the world to come must be transformed matter of this world. God will no more abandon the universe than he will abandon us. Hence the importance to theology of the empty tomb, with its message that the Lord's risen and glorified body is the transmutation of his dead body.[31]

Haught's more Whiteheadian take on Polkinghorne's reference to information theory is that God "remembers," or takes into God's own experiences, the patterns of events that constitute all living things throughout the sequences of their lives according to God's aim to achieve the maximum intensity of beauty and harmony both for God and for all sentient beings. In other words, God "resurrects" from these embodied processes "patterns of information" that constitute that new mode of existence to which the New Testament refers as the Kingdom of God.[32]

Buddhist Responses to Evolutionary Biology

According to standard Buddhist doctrine, the universe is "co-originated" because of the arising and passing away of various causes and conditions. Neither the universe nor human kind is the creation of a designing god. This is the heart of Buddhist nontheism. But Buddhist doctrines do not necessarily deny the existence of God or a plurality of gods in any blanket way. The point for Buddhists is that even if God or a plurality of deities truly exists, such beings cannot help persons achieve "Awakening." Suffering caused by clinging to the fiction of permanent selfhood is a human problem and demands a human solution, and God or gods are of no help; in fact, worshipping God is another from of clinging to an imaginary permanence that generates suffering. For this reason, most Buddhists conclude there can be in principle no conflict between Buddhism and science in general and between Buddhism and evolutionary biology in particular since Buddhism, like the natural sciences, rules out God as a meaningful explanatory category.

There is much truth to the widespread Buddhist opinion that Buddhism and the sciences are compatible. Nothing similar to the history of conflict that haunts certain forms of Christian theological reflection on evolutionary theory can be found in Buddhist history. Indeed, the general Buddhist opinion is that Buddhism and evolutionary biology share "common ground" on the very issues that some Christians have perceived as a threat to Christian faith and practice. In particular, when the natural sciences are stripped of materialist metaphysics, the conclusion that the defining doctrines of Buddhism are easily harmonized with contemporary scientific thought is an item of faith for many Buddhists.

The opinion of William S. Waldron seems typical of this view. "The dialogue is only possible," he writes,

> because recent developments in Western thought have begun to find common ground with traditional Buddhist perspectives on the human condition, including the underlying conditions of human evil. There is a growing consensus that we may understand ourselves and our world more deeply and fully if we may understand things in terms of interconnected patterns of relationships rather than as reified entities existing somehow independently of their own developmental history, their internally differentiated processes, or their enabling conditions. There exists, that is, an increasing recognition that thinking in terms of unchanging essences, entities, and identities deeply misconstrues the human condition—a misunderstanding that inadvertently leads to, rather than alleviates, human evil and suffering.[33]

Since most contemporary Buddhist reflection on the natural sciences assumes José Cabezón's "complementarity model," it will be helpful to describe briefly the most important elements of Buddhism's classical worldview that appear to be in harmony with contemporary science. I shall focus on Waldron's views as an illustration of this trend, supplemented by the views of other Buddhist writers.

Waldron's approach to dialogical encounter with biology is comparative in nature, as are the approaches of most Buddhists. According to standard Buddhist teaching, it is our confusion about the nature of the self that provides the central doctrinal focus of Buddhist conceptual dialogue with Christianity, as well as the natural sciences. At issue is the paradoxical nature of our experience of self-identity through time, meaning our experience of ourselves *as the same self* through the moments of our lives as we simultaneously experience that we are *not the same self* through the moments of our lives. Platonic notions of the self emphasized the stability of the experience of self-identity through time and asserted an unchanging, permanent, substantial self-entity called the "soul" that experiences change but itself neither undergoes change nor is affected by the changes of the body within which, in some sense, the soul dwells.

However, Buddhist doctrine rejects all notions of permanence in any form. Even the universe is impermanent because it, too, is constituted by nonself. Permanent self-identity through time—the experience of our selves as the same self through the moments of our lives—is an illusory social construction. Rather than being constituted by a permanent "soul," or self-entity, all things and events are constituted by an interdependent series of ceaselessly becoming relationships. Since the relationships that we undergo at any moment, which constitute our identity at that moment, are always in the process of change and becoming (i.e., they are "impermanent"), so, too, are all things and events in the universe impermanent. Thus, we are not "permanent selves" that *have* interdependent relationships; we *are* the interdependent relationships we undergo and experience as we continuously undergo and experience them. So, we are not permanent self-entities that "have" friendships, enemies, insight, ignorance, love, anger, stupidity, wisdom, family, or emotional states; we *are* our friendships, enemies, insight, ignorance, love, anger, stupidity, wisdom, family, or emotional states as we undergo and experience them. Since none of the interdependent relationships we constantly undergo and experience from moment to moment throughout our lives are permanent, neither are we permanent "selves." We are "nonselves" who are "empty" (śūnyatā) of permanent selfhood.

Waldron's approach is to move the Buddhist doctrines of nonself, dependent co-origination, and interdependence from the realm of Buddhist philosophy to an investigation of the impact on human lives caused by our tendency to reify our particular experience of self-identity through time into an independent, substantially permanent self-entity. In standard Buddhist teaching, permanent self-identity is a false construction whose source arises from "ignorance" (*avidyā*) about ultimate reality, meaning in Buddhism "the way things really are as impermanent." When we "cling" (*taṇhā*) to permanent selfhood, we live out of accord with reality, the karmic result of which is "unsatisfactoriness" and "suffering" (*duḥkha*), both for ourselves and for other living things. Release from suffering, the "Third Noble Truth," happens only when we realize that the impermanence we experience is a mirror image of the impermanence of the universe. For if there is nothing permanent to which to cling, like a permanent self-entity, the only alternative is to "let go" of permanent selfhood, an experiential realization engendered by the practice of meditation and called "Awakening" (*nirvāṇa*).

In relating Buddhist doctrine to evolutionary biology, Waldron asserts that both Buddhism and important aspects of contemporary science seem congruent because both teach that we may understand ourselves and the natural world more deeply if we conceive all phenomena, including ourselves, as interconnected patterns of relationships, rather than as permanent self-entities that exist independently of their own evolutionary histories.[34] However, while belief in an independent permanent self may be a dangerous mistake, it remains a practical "conventional truth" that, from the point of view of evolutionary biology, fulfills an important purpose in nature because it enhances human survival. In other words, belief in permanent selfhood must have historically had positive evolutionary advantages.

Here Waldron draws on the Madhyamika distinction between "absolute truth" and "conventional truth." According to Madhyamika epistemology, the absolute truth is that all things and events and the universe as a whole are "empty" of permanent, substantial self-identity through time. It is attachment to this conventionally created half-truth of permanent selfhood that constitutes the fundamental illusion that is the source of human suffering. But the "practical" or "conventional" truth is that our experience of independent self-identity is not a complete illusion because what we interpret as independent self-identity brings "practical" evolutionary benefits.[35] Or, in more specific Buddhist formulation, the actions engendered by belief in an independent self lead to reproductively successful results that strengthen the sense of independent selfhood, while simultaneously becoming the source of human-caused suffering. From a Buddhist point of view, it is only by experientially realizing, that is, waking up to, the constructed, illusory nature of all phenomena, including oneself, that we are liberated from all the mental afflictions that are the source of suffering for human beings. Here, Waldron concludes, exists a point of entry for dialogue and collaborative research between Buddhists and evolutionary biologists.

Waldron's drawing on Madhyamika thought is a common pattern in Western Buddhist dialogue with the sciences. I noted a similar pattern in the way Buddhists have encountered physics and cosmology in chapter 3. The distinction between absolute truth and conventional truth allows many Buddhists to portray scientific theory and discovery as partial, limited descriptions of what physically goes on in the universe. Scientific descriptions are instrumental truths that bring practical, beneficial technological applications that improve the quality of human life. But Madhyamika Buddhist epistemology leaves Buddhist claims about absolute truth untouched, thereby unchallenged, by scientific inquiry. Absolute truth and the secondary truths of scientific inquiry can be in harmony because secondary truths may be, and generally are, viewed as instrumental expressions of the absolute truth that is experienced only at the moment of Awakening. How, therefore, can evolutionary biology, stripped of the materialist metaphysics of writers like Richard Dawkins and E. O. Wilson, and Buddhism be in conflict?

In summary, the dialogical stance of most Buddhists engaged with evolutionary biology, as well as physics and cosmology, is appropriately characterized by Cabezón's complementarity model. The governing assumptions of the complementarity model require clarification. First, there are aspects of Buddhism's worldview that can be considered as "scientific" in some meaningful way, even though it is misleading to characterize Buddhism or any other religious tradition as "scientific." E. O. Wilson agrees with most working scientists in his definition of science as an organized, systematic enterprise that gathers knowledge about the universe and condenses this knowledge into testable laws and principles expressed mathematically.[36] This means that the natural sciences investigate objective networks of cause and effect across adjacent levels of physical organization characterized by an empirical methodology that stands in stark contrast to the methods and concerns of the humanities, including philosophy and theology.

Buddhism, too, according to the complementarity model, is concerned with causality *within* subjective human experience. In this sense, Buddhism is often described as a form of naturalism similar to that of the natural sciences (e.g., Buddhism is presented as a body of systematic knowledge that posits a wide array of testable hypothesis and theories concerning the nature of the mind and the mind's relation to the physical environment). In this sense, according to B. Alan Wallace, Buddhism may be characterized as a form of empiricism since Buddhist doctrines about the mind and mental experiences have been tested and experientially confirmed numerous times over the past twenty-five hundred years through the practice of meditation.[37]

Second, there are major differences between Buddhism and science that bear particular relevance to Buddhist dialogue with biology. One major difference between Buddhism and the natural sciences is that scientific method systematically excludes subjective experience from the natural world while attributing causal efficacy only to objective physical phenomena. In contrast, Buddhism, because of its emphasis on the practice of meditation, takes subjective mental phenomena as seriously as objective physical phenomena and posits a wide range of interdependent causal connections between them. Thus, it is said, Buddhism employs rigorous methods for investigating the necessary and sufficient causes of the subjective experience of suffering and happiness to a much greater extent than contemporary biology. The intention of Buddhist practice is not only to identify and counteract the causes of suffering before they arise. All conditioned phenomena arise from multiple causes, and the meditative practices that specialize on identifying the *interior subjective* causes of joy and sorrow are regarded by Buddhists to be more crucial than the *outer objective* physical causes of suffering. Wallace argues that this is the most "scientific" aspect of Buddhism because it addresses issues in human experience that are largely ignored by the methods employed by natural sciences.[38]

Summary Observations: Buddhism

The argument that Buddhism is more compatible with the biological sciences than Christianity seems to rest on a single conclusion operating as a presupposition. Since none of the teachings and practices of Buddhism presuppose the existence of a transcendent sacred reality that creates and directs the universe according to a divine plan, the sciences do not pose serious challenges to Buddhism's worldview in general or to Buddhist practice in particular. Accordingly, this argument goes, Buddhism and the sciences, particularly evolutionary biology, have a certain consonance that allows fruitful dialogue.

This claim does not normally mean that there are no differences between Buddhism and the natural sciences. For example, Buddhists like Waldron, Wallace, and the Dalai Lama usually interpret scientific conclusions established experimentally according to scientific method as true, yet "incomplete," objective descriptions of natural processes. Scientific method limits the practice of science to very limited bits of experience while excluding wider bodies of experience. This is the source of the power of scientific explanation, but it is also a limitation because, by ignoring most of the constituents of reality, science offers an incomplete account of "the way things really are." For this reason, many Buddhists conclude that scientific truths are "secondary truths" because they lead to important technological benefits. But the sciences need to be "deepened" by engagement with Buddhism, just as Buddhism needs to be "deepened" by contextualizing its teachings and practices through what the sciences reveal about natural processes.

The Buddhist point seems to be this: like Christianity, Buddhism asserts that reality is much deeper than the physical processes studied by scientific method. There exist subjective phenomena: the experience of self-consciousness and self-identity through time, mental and emotional experiences, memory of the past, anticipation of the future, fear, hope, and, for human beings, certain knowledge that all living beings will experience death. These subjective experiences do not seem reducible to the interplay of electrons, atoms, and molecules, at least for Buddhists and Christians. The specific Buddhist conclusion is that such subjective phenomena are either intentionally ignored by working scientists or explained away by scientists reading their conclusions through the filter of philosophical materialism. It is the practice of meditation, which is fundamentally an intense, empirical self-analysis of a wide array of subjective mental and emotional experiences, that not only reveals the cause of human suffering but also engenders release from suffering. It is personal discovery of the "absolute truth" that all objective and subjective things and events are "empty" of permanent self-existence that engenders Awakening.

Subjective experiences have a certain "objectivity" because of the long history of Buddhist methods of meditative investigation and observation. Of course, subjective mental experiences cannot be reproduced experimentally in a laboratory, but they are nevertheless observable by means of meditation, and they point directly to an absolute truth that is capable of unifying Buddhist knowledge of subjective interior phenomena with scientific knowledge of objective natural phenomena. It is here that Buddhism can contribute to the creative transformation of the sciences by offering a more complete picture of reality as a whole in place of focusing only on objective physical relationships reducible to mathematical description.

Not many working scientists, unless they are Buddhists, agree with this assessment of their work. Most scientists presuppose a "critical realist" stance: scientific conclusions bear some semblance to objective matter of fact but are always capable of revision as new experimental evidence is discovered that falsifies previous conclusions. But scientists do not regard their descriptions of natural phenomenon as "secondary truths" in need of completion by any religious tradition. Still, Buddhists make a valid point. The natural sciences are in fact currently unable to give a satisfactory account of subjective experience. The problem is not only the tendency of biologists to read their data through the screen of materialist metaphysics. Scientific methods as now constituted are simply incapable of explaining interior subjective experiences like self-awareness, our awareness of others, and self-identity through time. Scientific methods are only adequate for describing physical realities through the interaction of physical quanta, electrons, atoms, and molecules. Exactly how mental experiences—self-awareness, mind, emotions, self-identity, memory, hope, morality, beauty, altruism, or religious experience—emerge from processes that are physical remains a mystery.

However, a more serious problem with the conclusion that Buddhism and the sciences are compatible is more philosophical. Not only is the conclusion that scientific truths are secondary truths incompatible with the self-understanding of most working scientists, but it engenders an incoherency in contemporary Buddhist-science dialogue. When the views of one's dialogical partner (a scientist) are declared in advance to be "secondary," while one's own truth (Buddhist) is declared to be "absolute," the dialogue seems cut off at the knees before it can begin. This problem has not to this date been addressed in current Buddhist dialogue with the natural sciences.

Yet, it is equally clear that Buddhists do not normally experience evolutionary biology as a threat to Buddhist faith and practice, especially when Buddhists are socially engaged with human degradation of the environment. Resolving these issues requires knowledge of evolutionary biology as the scientific foundation of Buddhist environmental ethics. Accordingly, evolutionary biology has willingly been incorporated into Buddhist environmental engagement in a creatively transformative way.[39] Furthermore, the neurosciences and cognitive sciences are of particular interest to Buddhists as they reflect on the practice of mediation, the nature of the experience of self-identity through time, and the relation between mind and body. Finally, psychological conclusions regarding the role of emotions are also of interest to Buddhists given Buddhism's understanding of emotional attachment to permanence as the cause of human suffering. This aspect of Buddhist engagement with neuroscientific theory will be a topic in the next chapter.

Summary Observations: Christianity

I suspect the majority of Christian theologians have pursued a separatist response to evolutionary biology, particularly in its materialist interpretations. Such responses presuppose some form of Barbour's conflict model. Included here would be those who affirm literalist readings of the Bible, particularly of

Genesis 1 and 2. But materialists like Dawkins and Wilson are also separatists who employ literalist readings of the Bible as the foundation of their rejection of all notions of God and their assertion of atheism as the only defensible interpretation of reality since the publication of *Origin of Species*. For Dawkins, Wilson, and other scientific materialists, all religions, including Buddhism, are nothing more than illusory wish fulfillments that may have had survival value prior to Darwin but that have now been exposed as collective illusions. Obviously, any encounter between Christians and scientists following a separatist line is best described as a monologue. For both, fundamentalist Christian and scientific materialist, Christian tradition and evolutionary biology are experienced as mutually threatening.

But there is another theological stance, one in which it is admitted that evolutionary biology demands a reconfiguration of Christian experience of an infinitely compassionate God who is the creator, sustainer, and faithful liberator of all living beings, human and nonhuman. These theologians, illustrated in this chapter by Peacocke and Haught, affirm evolutionary biology in an intellectually serious way by recognizing that it is impossible to have exactly the same notions of God and God's action in the world after 1859. Such thinkers reject literalist interpretation of either the Bible or the natural sciences. They engage the sciences either from some version of Barbour's dialogue model or his integration model or a combination of the two. The resulting theological engagement is thoroughly dialogical with the aim of creatively transforming both Christian tradition and evolutionary biology. The general working principle supporting this more "liberal" form of theological reflection is the enrichment of our understanding of the universe as a means of clarifying and revitalizing Christian tradition's sense of divine providence in the universe. If Christianity is to flourish within contemporary culture, Christian understanding of just how God cares for every thing and event in the universe requires fresh expression by means of a kenotic evolutionary theology.

Typically, religious skeptics like Dawkins and Wilson ask how the idea of an intelligent and creative providence can be reconciled with the scientific fact of randomness and contingency in the evolution of life. Haught has perhaps the most thoughtful response to this question,[40] but one finds similar arguments in the work of Peacocke, Polkinghorne, Russell, and others. Indeed, contingency and randomness are facts of nature, but these facts teach Christians much about God's fundamental character, described by the writer of the First Letter of John as love. First, it is the nature of love to allow the beloved to exist without coercion. As we know from our own limited experiences, genuine love never forces or compels. Love allows others sufficient time to become themselves. So, if there is truth to the biblical notion that God cares for the universe as something other than God, than the universe must always possess some degree of autonomy, even during its long prehuman evolution. There has to be room for contingency and chance in any universe held to be both distinct from, yet loved by, God. The remorseless consistency of the laws of nature, including natural selection, are also essential to the relative autonomy with which the universe is endowed by its creator.

Furthermore, if the universe and its life-forms are really differentiated from God, considerable temporal duration is required for the pluralism of life-forms engendered by natural selection to evolve. The universe's creation did not take place in one magical instant 13.5 billion years ago or entail that evolutionary adaptation will be perfect. God's creative activity includes letting the universe be, not manipulative control over it. A coherent theology constrained by evolutionary biology may argue that God does not really care for the universe unless the universe is allowed in some sense to be self-actualizing within the boundary conditions of relevant possibilities provided to it by God. The enormous epochs of evolutionary history that reveal the emergence of life by random variation and natural selection are consistent with the idea of a God who loves the universe enough to allow it to become distinct from God.

In addition, a coherent evolutionary Christian theology of grace will argue that God could not really care for the universe unless the universe possessed its own forms of self-actualization. Love and compassion do not coerce the beloved. Rather, love's power is the power of persuasion, for human beings and for God. So, it is possible to read the entire history of the universe, including the features that seem to many human beings to render it absurd, as a story of an emerging freedom capable of increasing intimacy between God and all sentient beings and insentient realities. Or, as Haught argues, what a theology of evolution sees going on in the depth of natural processes "is the gift of God's own self-being poured into the creation, and the emerging creation being taken into the life of God."[41]

This style of theological reflection is known as "kenotic theology" and constitutes an important form of theological conversation with evolutionary biology. Kenotic theologies may assume a number of forms, but a common feature of most is that divine action in nature is understood as persuasive rather than coercive, a point that is particularly stressed in Christian process theology. According to evolutionary theory, the history of life percolates with contingency. If God's character is love rather than dominating force, the sentient beings that are the collective life of the universe must be allowed to evolve and to participate in the adventure of their own self-creation. If God

were a cosmic dictator, we might expect the universe to be a completed creation from the beginning and remain unchanged over billions of years of
time. The facts of evolutionary biology make this claim incoherent; when
"divine action" is conceived in biblical terms, however, it opens the universe
to an always-new future. The facts of evolution therefore challenge traditional Christian theology to extend the biblical sense of divine promise beyond the aspirations of Judaism and Christianity, beyond concern for human
history, out into the universe itself.

In other words, awareness of evolution is a means by which Christians
may broadly understand the scope of divine promise, as well as divine compassion. In this sense, reconstructing Christian theological reflection in dialogue with evolutionary biology will allow Christians to envision the story of
the universe and its life as a whole, not just life on earth, as taken into God's
own selfhood, where it is ultimately preserved and redeemed from all that human beings might consider to be absolute loss. The billion of years of evolutionary experimentation, suffering, and loss necessitated by natural selection
do not happen outside of God's own life and experiences. A major theme of
kenotic theology in dialogue with evolutionary biology is that God's loving
compassion empathetically embraces all the ambiguity and order in the universe as a means of redeeming all creation.

Finally, from a kenotic- and process-theological perspective, all scientific
descriptions of the physical structures of existence will of necessity constrain
how theologians should think about how God can be active in the universe.
As scientific theories change, so will the constraints placed on Christian theological reflection. Quantum theory, together with the indeterminacy of mi-
crosystems it entails, has attracted much attention for premise that if God is
active in all events, then God must be involved in the most fundamental of
events that occur in the quantum realm. Quantum mechanics is not predictive in the same sense as classical mechanics. While the trajectory of a rocket
can be predicted with precise accuracy, the location or spin-state of an elec-
tron cannot. Accordingly, Robert John Russell argues that this indeterminacy constitutes a "causal joint" whereby God can influence events in the
macro world without violating the laws of nature God creates.[42] However,
like all speculations of this sort, there are problems: it is not clear how God
could influence the behavior of electrons and atomic nuclei or, if God in fact
did, how this would influence macrosystems. For this reason, Philip Hefner
writes that "we ought to resist the temptation to move too easily from quan-
tum-talk to God-talk."[43]

Chaos theory has also been appropriated by theologians as a means of reflecting on the possibility of divine action. The chaotic behavior of many sys-

tems seems to offer a top-down, holistic mechanism by which God interacts with the world; God acts through influencing dynamic patterns through input of what Polkinghorne has referred to as "active information."[44] However, the issue here is that explanations of the behavior of chaotic systems are based on deterministic mathematical equations of nonlinear systems. For such systems to possess the sort of openness needed to create a "causal joint" through which God can interact with the universe, it is necessary to assume that these equations reflect a more subtle reality than the deterministic reality they describe. Polkinghorne admits that the details of this more subtle reality cannot at present be spelled out.[45]

Given the problems raised by interpreting divine action through the lenses of either quantum theory or chaos theory, Ross L. Stein, writing from a Whiteheadian process perspective, thinks it is best to think of divine action in three interdependently multiple modes: Chemical becoming/ quantum mechanics, chemical becoming/nonlinear dynamics, and quantum mechanics/nonlinear dynamics.[46] Yet, each of these perspectives has issues that require further reflection.

- *Chemical becoming/quantum mechanics.* Molecular systems can be described through quantum wave functions, and the chemical reactions of these systems can be described by a particular time dependence of the appropriate wave functions. The question is, does God influence the chemical becoming of molecular systems by influencing the evolution of their wave functions through time, and if so, how?
- *Chemical becoming/nonlinear dynamics.* Dissipative chemical systems are those that operate far from equilibrium and are thought to form the basis for the development and emergence of complexity. Does God influence the development of complexity at the level of the chaotic behavior of dissipative chemical systems, and if so, how?
- *Quantum mechanics/nonlinear dynamics.* Investigating the relationship between deterministic chaos and quantum mechanics is currently an area of intense research in physics. Some investigators are now exploring areas in which classical mechanics and quantum mechanics seem to overlap. However, quantum theory is still in the process of development, and there are many unanswered questions, including how to synthesize relativity theory with quantum theory. So, theologians who interpret divine action in terms of the chaotic behavior of quantum systems need to be aware that exactly how quantum mechanics reflects the chaos of classical mechanics, and vice versa, is incredibly uncertain.

The issues raised by each of these modes of divine action theory do not in themselves mean that science has illuminated the need to think of God as a creator who continues to be engaged with all things and events in the universe. In all probability, a coherent theological theory of divine action will have to incorporate aspects of each of these modes. Exactly how remains an open question, given the current state of research in the natural sciences that must constrain theological reflection.

Notes

1. The Copernican revolution began in 1543, the year of Nicolaus Copernicus's death, with the publication of his *De revolutionibus orbium celestium* (On the Revolution of the Celestial Spheres), along with the publication in 1687 of Isaac Newton's *Philosophiae naturalis principia mathematica* (The Mathematical Principles of Natural Philosophy). The theories and discoveries of Copernicus and Newton, as well as of Kepler, Galileo, and others, conceived of the universe as matter in motion governed by natural laws.

2. See Francisco J. Ayala, "The Evolution of Life," in *Evolutionary and Molecular Biology: Scientific Perspectives on Divine Action*, ed. Robert John Russell, William R. Stoeger, and Francisco Ayala (Vatican City: Vatican Observatory Publications and the Center for Theology and the Natural Sciences, 1998), 25. Also see Ayala's second essay in this volume entitled "Darwin's Devolution: Design without Designer," 101–16.

3. William Paley, *Natural Theology*, cited in Ayala, "The Evolution of Life," 24.

4. George V. Coyne, *Science and Theology: Ruminations on the Cosmos*, ed. Chris Impey and Catherine Petrey (Rome: The Vatican Observation and the Templeton Foundation, 2002), 26–27.

5. See Charles Birch's description of the interdependence of chance and necessity in Charles Birch and John B. Cobb Jr., *The Evolution of Life* (Denton, TX: Environmental Ethics Books, 1990), ch. 2.

6. Ayala, "The Evolution of Life," 27–29.

7. Langdon Gilkey, *Nature, Science, and Religion: The Nexus of Science and Religion* (Minneapolis: Fortress Press, 1993), 100.

8. Gilkey, *Nature, Science, and Religion*, 100.

9. Behe's best-known book is *Darwin's Black Box: The Biochemical Challenge to Evolution* (New York: Free Press, 1996), the publication of which is the beginning of the intelligent design movement.

10. For an extended critique of Behe's arguments for intelligent design, see John F. Haught, *Deeper Than Darwin: The Prospect Religion in an Age of Evolution* (Cambridge: Westview Press, 2003), 88–93.

11. Robert John Russell, "Intelligent Design Is Not Science and Does Not Qualify to Be Taught in Public School Science Classes," *Theology and Science* 3 (July 2005): 131–32.

12. For a wonderful history of the relationship between science and religion since the sixteenth century, see John Hedley Brooke, *Science and Religion: Some Historical Perspectives* (Cambridge: Cambridge University Press, 1991).

13. Arthur Peacocke, *Theology for a Scientific Age* (Minneapolis: Fortress Press, 1993), 19–23.

14. See Peacocke's keynote address published in the *Science and the Spiritual Quest* Boston conference program, October 21–23, 2001, titled "Science and the Spiritual Quest: Intersections for Today," 1–7.

15. Peacocke, *Theology for a Scientific Age*, 102.

16. Peacocke, *Theology for a Scientific Age*, 52–55.

17. Peacocke does not go as far with this model of God's interaction with the world as Sallie McFague because he thinks this notion runs the risk of ignoring Christian experience of God's nature as transcendent to the universe God's creates, much like an artist transcends a work of art, yet incarnates his or her intention and design in a work of art. See Sallie McFague, *Models of God: Theology for an Ecological, Nuclear Age* (Philadelphia: Fortress Press, 1987), 69–77.

18. That is, the strong and weak nuclear forces, electromagnetic force, and gravity.

19. Peacocke, *Theology for a Scientific Age*, ch. 11.

20. For a detailed description of the different theories of emergence, see Philip Clayton, *Mind and Emergence: From Quantum to Consciousness* (Oxford: Oxford University Press, 2004), ch. 1.

21. See Arthur Peacocke, *Evolution: The Disguised Friend of Faith?* (Philadelphia: Templeton Foundation Press, 2004), ch. 2.

22. John F. Haught, *God after Darwin: A Theology of Evolution* (Boulder, CO: Westview Press, 2000), 9.

23. Haught, *God after Darwin*, 37–38.

24. Haught, *God after Darwin*, 38.

25. See Pierre Teilhard de Chardin, *The Phenomenon of Man* (New York: Harper Torchbooks, 1961), 257–72.

26. Haught, *God after Darwin*, 38–39.

27. Haught, *God after Darwin*, 39–40.

28. Haught, *God after Darwin*, 42–43.

29. See Alfred North Whitehead, *Adventures of Ideas* (New York: The Free Press, 1967), 252–96, for Whitehead's notion that God's relation to the universe is best conceived as an "adventure" that "lures" all creation to new levels of intensity of experience.

30. Haught, *God after Darwin*, 42.

31. John Polkinghorne, *Belief in God in an Age of Science* (New Haven, CT: Yale University Press, 1998), 164.

32. For more extended discussions of Haught's understanding of redemption, see *God after Darwin*, ch. 5, and *Deeper than Darwin* (Cambridge: Westview Press, 2003), ch. 11.

33. See William S. Waldron, "Common Ground, Common Cause: Buddhism and Science on the Affliction of Society," in *Buddhism and Science: Breaking New Ground*, ed. B. Alan Wallace (New York: Columbia University Press, 2003), 146.

34. Waldron, "Common Ground, Common Cause," 155–64.

35. Waldron, "Common Ground, Common Cause," 164–71.

36. E. O. Wilson, *Consilience: The Unity of Knowledge* (New York: Knopf, 1998), 58.

37. B. Alan Wallace, *The Taboo of Subjectivity: Toward a New Science of Consciousness* (New York: Oxford University Press, 2000), 103–18.

38. B. Alan Wallace, "Introduction: Buddhism and Science," in *Buddhism and Science*, 8.

39. See, for example, the collection of essays edited by Mary Evelyn Tucker and Duncan Ryukan Williams, *Buddhism and Ecology: The Interconnection of Dharma and Deeds* (Cambridge, MA: Harvard University Press, 1997).

40. Haught, *Deeper than Darwin*, 78–83.

41. Haught, *Deeper than Darwin*, 79.

42. Robert John Russell, "Finite Creation without a Beginning: The Doctrine of Creation in Relation to Big Bang and Quantum Cosmologies," in *Quantum Cosmology and the Laws of Nature: Scientific Perspectives on Divine Action*, ed. Robert John Russell, Nancy Murphy, and C. J. Isham (Vatican City: Vatican Observatory Publications, 1993), 291–326.

43. Philip Hefner, "Editorial," *Zygon* 35 (2000): 467–68.

44. John Polkinghorne, "The Metaphysics of Divine Action," in *Chaos and Complexity: Scientific Perspectives on Divine Action*, ed. Robert John Russell, Nancy Murphy, and Arthur R. Peacocke (Vatican City: Vatican Observatory Publications, 2000), 147–56.

45. Polkinghorne, "The Metaphysics of Divine Action," 153–54.

46. Ross L. Stein, "The Action of God in the World—A Synthesis of Process Thought in Science and Theology," *Theology and Science* 4 (2006): 64–65.

CHAPTER FIVE

~

Buddhist-Christian Dialogue with the Cognitive Sciences

Scientific disciplines are interdependent in spite of each particular discipline's specialized focus. The collection of disciplines comprising the cognitive sciences is often perceived to have special relevance for Buddhists and Christians.[1] The reason seems obvious. The theoretical perspective and research of the cognitive sciences will directly affect how we think about the human person, from the nature of consciousness, to issues of freedom, to religious experience, to how we think about ourselves within the larger context of the natural world. This is so because the human mind appears connected to other minds through culture, our relation to other animals, and a common evolutionary past. For Christians, most obviously, the cognitive sciences will constrain how one thinks about God and God's relation to the world since Christians often think of God as a mind or a person.

While God is not an issue for Buddhists, the cognitive sciences require both Buddhists and Christians to rethink their worldviews and practice traditions. The nature of consciousness and mind are important areas of research and discussion, not only for the cognitive sciences but also for Buddhist philosophy and meditative practice, as well as for Christian theology and the practices of prayer and contemplation. In the monotheistic traditions, particularly in Christianity, the "signs of the spirit" in humanity—whether in the three-part anthropology of the New Testament (*sarx, psyche, pneuma,* or "flesh, soul, spirit") or in more dualistic accounts that have separated mind and body in Western thought since René Descartes—have long been taken as proof of God's existence and as evidence of the *imago dei* in humanity. The doctrine that human beings are "images of God" has, in turn, been a theological justification for sharply separating human beings from all other living beings, as well as for patriarchal separations of men from women, resulting in human exploitation of nature and male oppression of females. While philosophical dualism has not been a metaphysical assumption of Buddhist thought and practice, understanding the nature of self-awareness—mental experiences such as anger, hope, happiness, suffering, release from suffering, and the nature of mind—is of fundamental importance for Buddhists traditions of meditation. But for many Christians, the recent explosion of new knowledge of the brain, in large part due to powerful new brain-imaging techniques, has been perceived by many as a frontal attack on Christian tradition. Yet, while Buddhists have been quite open to the work of the cognitive sciences, this openness had not been without tensions arising from the materialistic metaphysics assumed by many important scientists working in the field.

It is important to understand why the neurosciences pose serious challenges for all religious traditions. The human brain is the most complicated biological structure that has evolved, at least as far as we know. The reason consciousness and cognition are so hard to describe is that human beings have evolved the capacity for self-knowledge, meaning a certain access to ourselves that gives us subjective experience, which in turn gives us a way of looking out at the world from where we are, as if we were on the inside looking out. This is extremely difficult to understand. Each one of us is trapped inside our brain, and therefore within a particular point of view and time, with the capacity to reflect on that particular point of view and time. But we can't get inside another person's brain, and no one else can get inside ours. So, the undeniable fact that we have particular perspectives is not closely paralleled with anything else we know about. The only thing we really know by experience in the whole universe is ourselves, but we are not sure about each other. This is the problem of other minds.

For Christian tradition, if there really exists a "ghost in the machine," as Gilbert Ryle described Descartes' notion of "spirit," then not only would the actions of this spirit "in" the brain be inaccessible to scientific study, but it would also imply the irrelevance of brain-based explanations of human thought and emotions. But the hard fact is that the cognitive sciences, particularly neuroscience, have achieved increasingly powerful explanations of human cognition, including detailed accounts of the physical relationships that underlie thought and emotions, with increasingly predictive ability. This means that the degree to which brain functions can be correlated with mentality will turn out to be much greater than anyone at present can currently imagine.

Of course, the neural correlates of consciousness do not in themselves, as Philip Clayton observes, prove that mind-body dualisms are false.[2] Yet, experimental evidence does suggest that consciousness is at least partly, perhaps largely, derived from a particular biological system, the brain and central nervous system, in interdependent interaction with physical, historical, cultural, and linguistic factors. So, here's the question: given the astonishing progress in understanding human thought and emotions in terms of the distributive neural systems of the brain, supported by an increasing ability to verify these theories with imagining techniques, must it be concluded that human cognitive functioning will be eventually fully accounted for in neurophysiological theory? And if so, does this not also constitute a challenge to Buddhist and Christian thought and practice because neuroscientific descriptions might well falsify all religious explanations of cognition and experience?

Most mainline Christian theological anthropology now rejects Cartesian dualism, and Buddhist tradition is based on a radically nondualistic worldview. Christian rejection of Cartesian dualism, which asserts a metaphysical difference between body and mind, has come at a price that Buddhists have not had to pay. Most theologians in dialogue with the cognitive sciences no longer think that it is possible to preserve the Cartesian distinction between mind and body, understood as two separate, but interacting, substances. The question for Christian theology is, what is the alternative? The most radical theological responses are linked to the work of neuroscientists Mary Hesse and Michael Arbib.[3] They argue that ideas may be theologically useful even after they have been fully correlated with physical processes within the brain and central nervous system since, from an evolutionary perspective, religious ideas have been useful for the survival of the human species. Somewhat following Hesse's and Arbib's lead, Nancy Murphy suggests that the human person may be understood in terms of "nonreductive physicalism" without abandoning the belief that human beings are the result of God's creative purposes and actions. That is, one can retain a Christian anthropology while abandoning all notions of soul or spirit, while espousing a physicalist interpretation of mind and brain.[4]

Such notions do not seem particularly useful to Philip Clayton. He points out that no one knows in advance what the "final" theory of cognition will turn out to be or that such a theory can be formulated in strictly neurophysiological or "physicalist" terms. "Not knowing, one is forced to *wager* on one outcome or the other."[5] Murphy's wager regarding cognition is with the core assumptions of physicalism. But Clayton wagers on the theory of emergence, which suggests that the explanatory principles and causes of each level of reality are distinct from, and not reducible to, lower levels. Thus, neurophysiological processes, contextualized by environmental influences, are interdependent aspects of the massively complex phenomena human beings experience as mentality, which will have elements unique to it that are not explainable in terms of its contributing physical causes. In the same vain, emergence theory wagers that religious experience will not be explained even by a complete understanding of human mentality since emergence theory is theoretically open to levels of reality beyond the human. What this "beyond" may be is a topic about which Christian theologians will have much to say.[6]

The theory of emergence has much to recommend it. Still, the issue is the question of whether emergence as an explanatory category really "explains" anything. For example, as the wetness of water cannot be attributed to the properties of the hydrogen or oxygen atoms in water molecules, thus is not reducible to the physical properties of molecules of hydrogen and oxygen, so the theory of emergence claims that cognition is not ingredient in the physical properties of the atoms and molecules of the human brain. Cognition is what "emerges" as a higher-order reality as the interactions of atoms and molecules become more and more complex. While emerging from these interactions, cognition cannot be reduced to these interactions. It is a higher-order reality. But the question is, is this an "explanation" of *how* cognition arises or merely the *description of an end result* of complex physical processes? The question is, how can physical processes give rise to nonphysical processes like self-awareness, hope, fear, or other forms of consciousness? Describing an end result of a process is not identical to describing how that process leads to an end result.

To see the issue regarding emergence theory clearly, it is necessary to summarize briefly current neuroscientific research on how the brain "works." This will be followed by some specific examples of ways in which Buddhists and Christians have encountered and appropriated this research in their doctrinal and practice traditions, followed by some conclusions in process.

The Mind Is What the Brain Does in a Biological and Environmental Context

The human brain is perhaps the most beautiful object that exists, at least on this planet, because it allows us to perceive beauty, experience a self that is in some sense self-identical through time while we are alive, and know something about the structure of existence. But how does the matter of the brain, which weighs about three pounds and has the consistency of curdled milk, bring into existence our capacity for self-reflection, emotional experiences, language, and the ability to "read" what is going on in the universe and in the minds of other people? What is the brain's relation to intellect, compassion, love, and hope or to more negative emotions like fear, anger, or hatred? How does a three-pound lump of meat connected to a central nervous system bring all this into existence? How does it bring into memory pleasant and unpleasant memories? Or allow us to anticipate the future?

The ancient Egyptians thought consciousness resided in the heart, so they scooped the brain out through the nose of a dead aristocrat before packing the emptied skull with a white cloth in a jar before burial. Likewise, the heart of the deceased was cut from the chest and placed in another jar with the corpse. The view that consciousness resides in the heart was shared by Aristotle and became the legacy of medieval philosophy and theology until the sixteenth century, when Descartes separated consciousness from the physical flesh of the brain. Cartesian dualism has exerted a powerful influence over Western science, philosophy, and theology for centuries. While dismissed by contemporary neuroscience, Cartesian dualism still feeds popular belief in the mind as a magical reality somehow not implicated in the biochemical processes going on in the brain. Yet, a contemporary of Descartes, Thomas Willis, was the first to suggest not only that the brain was itself the locus of the mind, but that different parts of the brain give rise to specific cognitive functions. Neuroscientists often refer to Willis as the father of neurology.

Early cognitive scientists by and large assumed that the mind could be studied in isolation from the biology of the brain. The idea was that since the mind was understood to be something like the "software of the brain," many early cognitive scientists perceived the mind as something very similar to Descartes' *res cogitans*, a nonextended, thinking thing that depended only incidentally on the biological process of the brain and the evolutionary properties of living organisms. Seen from this point of view, it was thought that the mind could be studied in isolation from its biological context, which provided only the physical structure that allowed the mind to function. But discoveries in the last forty years employing powerful imaging techniques for visualizing the regions within the brain for thought, emotion, and behavior are now revolutionizing scientific understanding of brain processes and the mentality these processes seem to generate.

The consensus of this research is that both the architecture of the human brain and the evolutionary history that has made the skulls we possess optimal for survival are significant for understanding who we are as persons and why we think and behave in the distinctive ways human beings do. Furthermore, the significance of the brain is only part of the general consensus of neuroscientists at the moment. It is now increasingly clear that a full understanding of the human mind requires an integrative approach that acknowledges not only that we have minds because we have brains and a central nervous system but that the mind/brain itself is intricately tied to the biology of our bodies, as well as to our physical and social environment. We are neither simply "minds" nor simply "brains." We are, as Gregory R. Peterson phrases it, "mind/brains." One cannot be understood apart form the other.[7]

Isolating the mind/brain from its wider biological and environmental contexts is a form of dualism described in Whiteheadian process philosophy as "the fallacy of misplaced concreteness." The interdisciplinary nature of contemporary neuroscience collectively, if not individually, tries to avoid this fallacy by generally focusing on mind/brain interdependence within the wider history of evolution (e.g., the role of genes in human mentality) and other biological and social contexts. Considered from this wider set of interdependent contexts, Peterson concludes,

> a brain alone does not produce a mind, let alone a person. To speak of the mind and, even more clearly, to speak of a person, is to move beyond the brain alone and into a complex web of relationships. The spinning of a person is less like a printed book and more like a conversation, less like a program and more like a network.[8]

Similarly, Gerald Edelman's argument that brain development is a Darwinian process supports Peterson's observation.[9] Shortly after birth, brain development is characterized by a massive die-off of neurons, the apparent reason for this being that we are born with far more neurons than we need. During our early years, the brain is literally "writing" and "programming" itself. Those neuron groups that end up operating functionally survive. Those that do not function die off. In turn, this fact implies that the physical and social environment plays an extremely important role in mental development, much of which occurs during the first three years of life. Recent evidence also suggests that brain development continues throughout adolescence, when areas of the brain associated with foresight and planning are not fully developed in teenagers until the early to mid-twenties, a fact to which any parent can attest.

Mapping brain functions requires incredibly sophisticated tools. One such tool is the electroencephalograph, which neuroscientists use to analyze electric currents given off by neurons as they "fire." The "Darwinian process" described by Edelman's work can be exemplified by considering the following "mapping" of a "simple" sensory event like seeing a snake. From the retinas in our eyes, the snake's image travels along the optic tract to the visual cortex where a "map" of the image is produced. The components of this image— its color, form, orientation—are segregated as they are processed along the temporal lobe, where the shape of perceived objects, in this instance, a snake is generated. These processes tell us *what* has been seen.

The frontal eye field then tracks *where* the snake is, directing eye movements and attention. The parietal cortex also receives input and provides information on the snake's position. This information is used to plan an action toward the snake. The hippocampus then consolidates long-term memories and emotional content crucial for making decisions. Like the principal server on a computer network, it integrates information coming from the visual cortex with input from other senses with *stored memories*— past experiences with snakes and learned cultural evaluations of snakes— resulting in full recognition of the snake. Finally, the amygdala immediately receives a first crude impression of the snake before the visual areas confirm its identity. This perception elicits an initial fear reaction, if one has learned to fear snakes. Fractions of a second later, the visual cortex, temporal cortex, and hippocampus send precise information about the snake, confirming the initial reaction.[10]

Of course, the multiplicities of conscious experience are much more complex than the simple sense impression of a snake. However, the imaging of brain activity of a variety of experiences seems to make it incontrovertible that the brain is the organ of the mind and consciousness. It is the only organ of the body that causes mental impairment when damaged. Since the brain is comprised primarily of neurons, and since neurons seem to function as dynamic conveyors of information, most cognitive scientists understand the activities of the mind primarily in terms of information processing. The question is, does the brain's information processing connect to the external world of sense objects. That is, does the brain connect us to a world ontologically independent of, or at least distinguishable from, how the mind/brain "reads" and "processes" information from sources external to the brain itself?

Of course even illusions are generated by the mind/brain for a number of reasons—brain damage, drugs, the limitations of experience, or other environmental factors. Persons do hear and see objects in the world that are not there to be seen or heard, although often this cannot be determined with certainty. Philosophically speaking, the brain generates both truth, however defined, and illusion, also however defined, which leads to an epistemological issue: how do we determine whether or not our mind/brain is deceiving us about the structure of the objective world? Moreover, how can we determine whether or not the minds/brains of other persons who publicly disclose what their minds/brains inform them of about the world is true or illusory?[11]

For religious persons, these epistemological issues are of great importance. Yet, strangely enough, a primary obstacle to the study of religious experience by cognitive scientists during much of the twentieth century has been acknowledging its existence, as many of them have relegated it to the category of pathology. William James was an exception. He criticized the medical materialists of his day who, for example, attributed St. Paul's conversion experience to epilepsy and who reduced religious experience to the workings of various glands.[12] Many contemporary neuroscientists still remain rooted in materialist assumptions such as these. But the general consensus of most is that, like all human experience, religious experience is generated by the physical processes of the human mind/brain interacting interdependently with cultural factors and the evolutionary history of human beings.[13]

Religious experience both unifies and divides Christians and Buddhists, one reason for this being that the term *religious experience* is itself vague, as can be seen by any survey of the extremely varied firsthand accounts given by individuals of their perceived religious experiences. These accounts indicate that not all religious experiences easily fit into a single framework. Religious experience, like all experience in general, is pluralistic in structure, which in turn makes neuroscientific descriptions extremely difficult. For Buddhists and Christians the pluralism of religious experiences also makes the philosophical and theological task of conceptualizing the structure of reality extremely difficult as well. Yet, neuroscientific research on religious experience has the potential of providing Christian and Buddhist thought with an empirical foundation not normally perceived by scientists or Buddhists or Christians. The fact that religious experiences may or may not confirm the specific truth claims of religious people has not been lost on Buddhist or Christian scholars, although a number of Christian writers have pointed out that theological claims do not rely solely on such experiences.[14] But neurobiological research into religious experience might provide a foundation for interior interreligious dialogue that is often lacking in conceptual and socially engaged dialogue.

But does experience, religious or otherwise, prove anything other than that one is having an experience generated by the mind/brain? More specifically, does religious experience connect us with anything real, independently of the physical processes of the mind/brain? In short, are the realities persons claim to experience during times of meditation and prayer ontologically there to be experienced? If so, how can such claims be verified? Do the religious claims of different traditions point to reality? Do the claims and practices of all religious traditions correspond to reality equally, but in their own distinctive ways? Does one religious tradition and set of practices correspond to reality more fully than the rest? How, indeed, can answers to these questions be determined one way or another?

Such questions are extremely complex and capable of only provisional answers, given the current state of research in the cognitive sciences. While these questions are not the specific concern of this chapter, they remain in the background for the following descriptive account of how Buddhists and Christians have dialogically engaged the neurosciences.

Buddhist Dialogue with the Cognitive Sciences

For twenty-five hundred years, Buddhists have employed strict training techniques to guide their mental states away from destructive emotions toward a more compassionate, happier frame of mind. Encouraged by thirty years of physical evidence of the brain's plasticity, cognitive scientists are now taking a keen interest in how meditation can change the mind/brain. For the past several years, for example, Richard Davidson at the University of Wisconsin, Madison, has been studying the brain activity of Tibetan Buddhists monks, in both meditative and nonmeditative states. Davidson had earlier demonstrated that people who are inclined to fall prey to negative emotions display a pattern of persistent activity in the right prefrontal cortex. In those with more positive temperaments, the activity occurs in the left prefrontal cortex. When Davidson ran the experiment on a group of senior Tibetan monks skilled in meditation, the monks' baseline activity was much further to the left than anyone had previously demonstrated.

Davidson also recently tested the prefrontal activity of volunteers from a high-tech company in Wisconsin. One group of volunteers received eight weeks of training in meditation, while the control group did not. All the participants received flu shots. By the end of the study, those who had meditated showed a pronounced shift of brain activity to the left prefrontal cortex. The group of meditators also showed a healthier immune response to the flu shot, suggesting that training in meditation affected the body's health, as well as the mind.[15]

A number of experiments monitoring brain waves using the electroencephalograms of individual Zen Buddhist monks and nuns during sessions of meditation have also been performed. Brain waves are a measure of the aggregate activities of large groups of neurons within areas of the brain that allow researchers to detect broad patterns of activity during specific kinds of activities. In one of the more widely known experiments on Zen monks, it was discovered that meditational states correspond to distinct brain-wave patterns and that transitions into more advanced stages of meditation can be correlated with further brain-wave changes.[16] For example, the research of M. Kasamatsu and T. Harai focused on twenty-three Zen Buddhist monks during meditation. They found each monk went through a series of four distinct stages during each meditation session, beginning with alpha waves, typical of both inward focused attention and deep relaxation, and ending for advanced meditators with theta waves, which are usually associated with drowsiness and hypnotic states. Only those who had meditated for more than twenty years showed theta wave activity. Also, the Zen master who guided the monks' practice could accurately distinguish between those monks who were at different meditational states without resorting to brain-wave data.[17] Barring the existence of extrasensory perception, the Zen master was quite able to discern the achievements in his students' practice because of his own years of rigorous training in meditation.

Of course, these experimental results neither prove nor disprove Buddhist claims about Awakening or that Awakening is reducible to brain states. I know of no Buddhist teacher who makes such claims. But brain-imaging research does suggest that disciplined practice of meditation over time can lead to kinds of experience that are, to some degree, quantifiable. In the case of Zen practice, prolonged meditation leads to distinctive patterns of brain activity, and these patterns probably correlate with specific kinds of experiences. One possible implication of this experimental result is that religious experiences produced by the practice of meditation are not merely the result of cultural conditioning, as claimed by Stephan Katz.[18] If religious experiences are purely a cultural construct, the sort of physiological states that are observed during prolonged periods of meditation should not matter. It appears to be the case, however, that cultural context over time produces new physiological states, which in turn lead to new cultural possibilities. That is, levels of human experience turn out to be biologically and culturally interdependent.

This may be one reason that most contemporary Buddhists do not normally experience the cognitive sciences as a threat but as empirical evidence that supports the positive benefits of the practice of meditation. Many Buddhists, for example the Dalai Lama, also conclude that this same evidence empirically confirms the truth of the doctrines of impermanence, nonself, and dependent co-origination. This is certainly a prominent theme among Buddhists in the Tibetan lineages, but Buddhists from other traditions, such as the Zen and South Asian Theravada traditions, generally concur. Three examples from the Tibetan tradition will suffice to illustrate this tendency.

The Dalai Lama argues that since its beginnings, Buddhist practice has always stressed careful observation and rational analysis of experience, as opposed to Christian tradition's reliance on "faith alone," which he tends to equate with "belief" in opinions without sufficient evidence to warrant that what one believes is "knowledge," a common mischaracterization, even among Christians.[19] Both Buddhism and science, particularly the neurosciences, he writes, are fundamentally pragmatic approaches to reality: one seeks knowledge in order to transform the mind and achieve freedom from suffering and its source from oneself. But this kind of self-transformation cannot be brought about by technology or scientific theories about the nature of physical reality, which he regards as "secondary truths" that are often disjointed from the absolute truth that constitutes Awakening. The transformation that creates the experience of Awakening can only be brought about by the mind. Moreover, the very possibility of the attainment of an Awakened mind is due to the impermanent nature of the mind itself and the fact that positive and unwholesome mental states arise from prior causes and conditions. Therefore, Buddhist understandings of the mind are naturalistic: the mind itself is an integral part of nature, and changes in the mind take place because of prior causes. In other words, from the perspective of Buddhism's worldview, the cognitive sciences in particular seem supportive of Buddhist doctrines and practices.

David Galin, a psychiatrist associated with the Tibetan lineage of Buddhism, arrives at similar conclusions but from a different direction than the Dalai Lama.[20] He argues that the "chaotic state" of Western accounts of the human self, particularly those in the neurosciences, are inadequate from the standpoint of Buddhist practice and doctrine. He points to the cognitive structure underlying day-to-day speech as a means of demonstrating that abstract thought is constructed of metaphors drawn from the elementary experiences of sensory perception and bodily movement. This creates large numbers of metaphoric systems, of which the world's religious traditions are examples, which in turn creates paradoxes in regard to ideas of the self and personhood. However, reframing concepts of self and person through the filter of Madhyamika philosophy can, he claims, resolve these paradoxes because this stream of Buddhist philosophy bears some correlation with the experimental results of neuroscientific studies of the human mind.

Finally, Matthieu Ricard, who has been a Buddhist monk for twenty years and who is one of the main French interpreters for the Dalai Lama, argues that the discoveries of mind/brain correlations via Western brain-imaging technology depend not only on the third-person observations typical of scientific method but also on the "first-person" observations of mental processes that Buddhists experience through their practice of meditation. The lack of first-person perspective in the cognitive sciences creates, he argues, an incoherency that can only be overcome by including the first-person perspectives of Buddhists disciplined in the practice of meditation in scientific accounts of consciousness. On the other hand, Buddhism lacks a "third-person perspective" because of its emphasis on first-person meditative experience.[21] For this reason, Ricard calls for the creation of a "contemplative science" that unifies the third-person theoretical descriptions of neuroscientific theory with first-person descriptions of mental states experienced by persons disciplined in meditation.

For Ricard, of course, Buddhist traditions of meditation are the primary model of a contemplative science because the fundamental purpose of Buddhist meditation is to understand the mind through direct, personal experiences of its mental content. The purpose of such immediate first-person experience is to purify the meditator's mind of "afflictions," such as "craving for permanence," hatred, and deluded self-centeredness, in order to discover by experience that state of genuine well-being Buddhists refer to as "Awakening." The well-being of Awakening is not a stimulus-driven pleasure, nor an intellectual or aesthetic joy, but a way of flourishing that emanates from the deepest nature of reality itself. Or, stated differently, the "pure awareness" that characterizes Awakening is an experience of transcending self-centeredness that opens persons to a deep sense of interdependence and altruism.

This implies that a contemplative science, particularly one based on Tibetan Buddhist traditions, is every bit as rigorous as the cognitive sciences and simultaneously more complete because the cognitive sciences typically leave out the subjective accounts of persons regarding their mental experiences. Buddhist tradition presents precise models for the observation of interior mental states, as well as a wide array of experiments, conducted for generations of practitioners, that have yielded repeatable results. Consequently, first-person mental experiences have given Buddhist doctrines an empirical foundation every bit as rigorous as third-person scientific description of mental states. Uniting the cognitive sciences with Buddhist teaching and practice into a contemplative science will, Ricard concludes, overcome the gaps in both the neurosciences (the lack of first-person descriptions) and Buddhist doctrine and practice (the lack of objective third-person descriptions).

In summary, two observations seem relevant in regard to Buddhism's general dialogue with the cognitive sciences. First, Buddhist tradition does not normally define itself as a "religion" or a "science." Consequently, one usually finds Buddhists claiming that scientific truths and Buddhist doctrines and practice are in harmony. Furthermore, the Dalai Lama voices the opinion of most Buddhist leaders when he declares that if compelling scientific evidence refutes any of the traditional doctrines of Buddhism, Buddhists should abandon these discredited teachings and their accompanying practices. The root of this attitude is the Buddhist belief that sentient beings are subject to suffering because of ignorance and delusion, and the way to the freedom that is experienced in Awakening lies in apprehending reality as it is. Accordingly, if scientific research reveals errors in Buddhist doctrine, Buddhists should be grateful for such scientific assistance in their particular pursuit of truth. This is why most Buddhists flatly reject the notion that Buddhism and science are nonoverlapping magisteria. Equally, Buddhists reject the postmodernist notion that Buddhist teachings are not subject to verification or change but rather consist simply of metaphors whose appeal is primarily aesthetic. This is the primary assumption underlying Buddhist dialogue with the natural sciences in general and the cognitive sciences in particular.

Second, scientific engagement with Buddhism can shed light on our own subjectivity, our own language, along with abstract categories such as religion, science, and philosophy. Through recognizing the uniquely specific contexts of both Buddhism and the cognitive sciences, all participants in Buddhist dialogue with the natural sciences may find a way of escaping the tendency to attribute privileged status to their own preconceptions, even if these are Buddhist—surely critically important for the practice of any sort of dialogue.[22]

Christian Encounter with the Cognitive Sciences

While scientists such as Donald MacKay and James Ashbrook provided early models of dialogue between religion and the cognitive sciences, it is only within the past two decades that a serious body of literature focusing on religious experience has been established that is reflective of this dialogue.[22] A few writers, like Richard Dawkins, E. O. Wilson, or Francis Crick, one of the codiscoverers of DNA, assert an ontological reductionism, meaning that all human cognitive functions, including religious experience, can be fully explained as the result of the physical interactions of atoms, molecules, genes, and neurons. Most, like McKay and Ashbrook, assert for a kind of "soft reductionism," meaning that religious beliefs and attitudes are reducible to biology, brain, and psychology, but this functions as a reason to encourage continued practice of religion as a natural human activity because it has aided the survival of the human species. Theirs is an epistemological reductionism claiming that the cognitive sciences are the only source of theological knowledge, but it is not necessarily an onto-logical reductionism that rejects claims that religious experience refers to anything ontologically real or that God does actually exists.[23] From this point of view, the most coherent conclusion about religious realities is agnosticism. Eugene d'Aquili and Andrew Newberg have also taken the path of soft reductionism by coining the term *neurotheology* to describe their work.[24]

From the particular standpoint of the cognitive sciences, human beings are the most complex organisms in the universe of which we are aware. While much has been discovered about our species, much remains un-known. So, while experimental research in the cognitive sciences does pro-duce specific, testable, and repeatable results, in the end the cognitive sci-entists can only provide working models and theories that interpret their research in ways that make their significance plain. It is, for instance, one thing to record the responses from split-brain patients and quite another to explain why these patients behave the way they do. As in other natural sci-ences, theories in the cognitive sciences rely on prior philosophical com-mitments that may or may not or conflict with the theological claims of Christian teaching and practice.

Among fundamentalist and many evangelical and neo-orthodox theolo-gians, the claims of the cognitive sciences are frequently seen as a chal-lenge to theology because they seem to call into question traditional doc-trines and formulations. In its strong form, this challenge may lead to conflict. Theological critics who still maintain a supernatural soul/body du-alism are likely to feel quite threatened by the cognitive sciences. More of-ten, scientific challenge serves as a goad for theologians to reexamine and reconsider the meaning of particular doctrines, which is the general ap-proach of those regarding themselves as neurotheologians. Sometimes this may result in doctrinal change, and sometimes not. For example, the reem-phasis on the doctrine of the resurrection of the dead, as opposed to the im-mortality of the soul, among many liberal Christian theologians (especially process theologians and others involved in the science-religion dialogue) may be one area where scientific findings have led theologians to a partic-ular path of reinterpretation.[25]

Exploring how the cognitive sciences often serve as a lens for theologi-cal reflection on a number of distinctive Christian doctrines is a central question in the work of Eugene d'Aquili and Andrew Newberg, who, as I have noted, coined the term *neurotheology*. According to their theoretical approach, the mind functions through a filter of seven "cogitative opera-tors," which are somewhat analogous to Immanuel Kant's categories, that act on the information the brain continually receives: (1) the holistic op-erator, (2) the reductionist operator, (3) the causal operator, (4) the ab-stractive operator, (5) the binary operator, (6) the quantitative operator, and (7) the emotional operator.[26]

The causal operator, for instance, is responsible for seeking out causal re-lationships, and the reductionist operator analyzes an object or an idea in terms of its parts, while the contrasting holistic operator tries to perceive parts as part of a larger whole, or gestalt. D'Aquili and Newberg describe these cognitive operators as located in specific areas of the brain, although the evidence for some of the cognitive operators, such as the emotional op-erator identified with the limbic system, is better than others, such as the bi-nary operator, which they do not assign to any location in the brain.

According to d'Aquili and Newberg, these cognitive operators give a complete account of the brain's cognitive functions, and thereby they ex-plain many forms of religious experience and symbolic expression. The work of the anthropologist Claude Levi-Strauss, who theorized that the function of mythology is the resolution of opposites, bears some resem-blance to d'Aquili and Newberg's theory. They claim that mythic narra-tives are a construct of the binary operator, while ritual is an attempt to re-solves these polarities. The resolution of polarities, whether in myth, ritual, or meditation, is called apophatic experience by Michael Sells.[27] Apophatic mystical experiences have a common structure in which the mystic loses all awareness of differentiation between a subject who experi-ences and an object that is experienced. D'Aquili and Newberg refer to such experiences as absolute unitary being (AUB), which occur cross-cul-turally.[28] Unlike Sells, they regard AUB as the primary form of religious ex-perience, while Sells's work also pays closer attention to forms of religious experience in which subject-object awareness does not disappear at the moment of experience, referred to by scholars of mysticism as "cataphatic experience." D'Aquili and Newberg do not concern themselves with cat-aphatic forms of religious experience to any significant degree.

The core element of d'Aquili and Newberg's theory that has attracted the most discussion is their account of how AUB arises in the brain. Activ-ities such as ritual and meditation work toward achieving various levels of AUB by causing a cascade of events that stimulate emotional pathways at the same time that areas in the parietal lobe of the cerebral cortex associ-ated with special orientation are cut off in a process called "differentiation." Since the parietal lobe is involved with spatial awareness and self-other distinctions, blocking off these areas would, they claim, result in the emergence of a mystical state, or AUB. Differentiation is said to occur as the result of overstimulation of the sympathetic and parasympathetic systems in the brain, which are, according to d'Aquili and Newberg, responsible for states of arousal and quiescence. Normally, these two systems compete with one another. However, religious activities, such as repetitive ritual dancing or focused meditation, often result in a kind of spillover effect that activates both systems. Differentiation, they claim, is the result that activates a conscious state of AUB.[29]

To test their theory, d'Aquili and Newberg ran an experiment on eight Tibetan Buddhist monks experienced in meditation. In each instance, when a meditator had attained an advanced meditational state, he was injected with a radioactive compound that highlighted brain areas by the blood flow at the time of injection. They interpreted more blood flow as greater brain activity and less blood flow as less brain activity. Twenty minutes after injection, each monk was given a Single Photon Emission Computed Tomography (SPECT) scan to image the radioactivity in the brain. When compared to the initial baseline scans, the results were consistent with their theory, showing, in particular, decreased activity in the left parietal lobe of each monk.[30]

What are the religious and theological implications of the results of this research? There is much controversy among theologians and cognitive scientists regarding d'Aquili and Newberg's research. However, it should be noted that they are more careful than many cognitive scientists in avoiding an ontological reductionism that denies the existence or reality of what meditators experience. *Something* is experienced, and the debate is about *what* is experienced. The nature of the "what" of religious experiences is always a matter of religious-theological interpretations that are always constrained by the specific histories, traditions, and cultural factors that are part of every religious tradition's distinctive worldview. The cognitive sciences can neither support nor deny the interpretative claims of any religious tradition, even if it can be absolutely demonstrated that AUB experiences are generated by the same physiological processes in the brain in all human beings, independently of cultural and historical contexts. Consequently, the fact that there are brain states that correlate with the experience of AUB does not mean that AUB does not exist or that the insights it generates when religious persons interpret their meaning are false. All conscious experiences involve brain states of one sort or another, so that whatever mode of consciousness we experience will have correlative brain states.

If this is true, then d'Aquili and Newberg's conclusion that normal states of consciousness should not be privileged over forms of religious consciousness engendered by the practice of meditation, ritual, or prayer seems valid. Such experiences may well be a means of attaining genuine insight into the structures of reality that are typically cloaked during normal experience. Accordingly, d'Aquili and Newberg argue that God and religion are integral parts of human experience and that the biological roots of religious experience in brain activity explain why, to the dismay of materialists like Wilson, Crick, and Richard Dawson, religious beliefs have not only not disappeared but, in fact, have experienced a worldwide resurgence in the late twentieth and early twenty-first centuries.[31]

This being said, it is also clear that d'Aquili and Newberg's work suggests that brain states are the primary causal agents in the formation of religious experiences like AUB. It is this point, of course, that stimulates Buddhist dialogue with the cognitive sciences, since Awakening as an AUB experience (according to d'Aquili and Newberg) is something that is pursued by an individual meditator's self-discipline and effort. For Christian tradition and practice, the question of the causation of religious experiences is of greater importance since religious experience is usually understood to have God as its source. In other words, Buddhist nontheism seems to fit more tightly with d'Aquili and Newberg's research than Christian monotheism. However, d'Aquili and Newberg have performed SPECT scans on Franciscan nuns during prayer. Here, the SPECT scans showed differentiation in the parietal lobe, which they claimed confirmed that the nuns experienced a form of AUB during intense focused prayer.[32]

If such scans do in fact reveal the physical component of religious experience defined as AUB, should we conclude that what shows up on the SPECT scans does not support the claim that God is the source of religious experience in the minds of the nuns at prayer? Are such experiences merely self-generated by the concentration and verbalization that is normally part of prayer? The scans of the nuns' brains indicated heightened activity in the forebrain and verbal association areas, but this is to be expected in any verbal task. Without a control group, it is not possible to know with certainty whether this pattern is distinctive. Moreover, since prayer is not always accompanied by AUB experience—a fact attested to by most Christians—it remains unclear how the data gathered by d'Aquili and Newberg about Franciscan nuns at prayer should be interpreted

Still, research such as d'Aquili and Newberg's raises important questions about how we should think about religious experience. A neurological foundation for religious experience seems to engender a bit of a paradox for Christians as well as for Buddhists: as neurological research confirms the reality of religious experience, it simultaneously threatens to undermine Buddhist and

Christian claims about its nature and cause. As Peterson notes, d'Aquili and Newberg's work is preliminary and raises as many questions as it resolves, a trait shared by all neurological research on religious experience at present. "For instance," Peterson asks,

> Would damage to the left parietal lobe affect a meditator's ability to achieve states of enlightenment? Are such experiences truly cross-cultural, suggesting a potential unifying principle to religions after all? Perhaps more to the point: is this all there is to it?[33]

The most that can be said at this point is that cognitive scientific research on religious experience is still in its infancy, and perhaps a healthy agnosticism regarding the correlation of brain states with religious interpretations about the nature of the objects the brain experiences is the most viable approach for now.

A Concluding Summary in Process

Given the fact that scientific research on religious experience is still in its infancy, conclusions must be tentative. The data is quite limited, and much more research needs to be done before any scientific account can be authoritative and comprehensive. Still, early research in the cognitive sciences does in fact pose an important question about how religious experience should be understood and exactly how religious experience is manifested in the brain. The claim that religious experiences are *merely* a derivative of culture is inadequate because biochemical processes within the brain also appear to play a causal role. Simultaneously, however, experiments within the cognitive sciences do not show that cultural elements are not part of religious experience, because achieving meditational states of experience through deep prayer or meditation requires significant preparation, training in specific techniques, and discipline of the intellect through doctrine—all aspects of culture. It remains true that religious persons experience what their particular traditions train them to expect to experience *even as* biochemical causal factors are at work in human brains.

So, while research like that of d'Aquili and Newberg can offer coherent scientific accounts of experiences of unity and bliss that mystics in all religious traditions have reported, it does not support stronger religious claims about the origin and significance of these experiences either in Buddhism or in Christianity. From a purely cognitive scientific standpoint, there remains plenty of room to interpret AUB experience as either an experience of Awakening or of the love of God. The question is always, what exactly do such experiences reveal about reality?

There appear to be at least three possible interpretations of the evidence thus far gathered. First, one could argue that the existence of brain states that correlate with AUB demonstrates that these experiences do not point to anything objectively real other than the biochemical processes of the brain. They are then essentially illusory states that are no different from states induced by drugs or brain damage. While scientific materialists most often draw this conclusion, d'Aquili and Newberg argue that the correlation of brain states with certain kinds of religious experience does not prove that these experiences are true or false or that religious experiences are necessarily delusional, in spite of the fact that any experience can be delusional.

Second, this acknowledgment does not establish that religious experiences such as AUB connect us to a sacred reality existing independently of our experiences that is named differently by different religious traditions, but it is also false to conclude that they do not.[34] Certainly it may well turn out that brain states are purely natural processes possessing no objective or "supernatural" component. Experience, including religious experience, does not interpret itself. What is needed, therefore, is a larger religious framework than religious traditions at present possess based on multiple considerations, in which biological, cultural, and historical considerations will play contributing roles. Such an interpretative framework might provide an account of powerfully transformative experiences within the broader context, in this case, of Buddhist and Christian practice, doctrine, and cultural-historical contexts. This, in turn, may provide fresh avenues for the practice of interreligious dialogue. If experiences like AUB are universal, which is the stance of students of mysticism like Michael Sells, and if they are understood to give genuine insight into the nature of reality, we might finally have one common foundation for interreligious dialogue.

The "ifs" at the end of the last paragraph raise the possibility of a third option. One could argue that brain states correlating with religious experience are not sufficient grounds for understanding religious experience. In this case, the argument might be that these experiences have a characteristic nature beyond what is reported by neuroscientific research. It is possible that some forms of Hinduism and Buddhism might find this position congenial. According to some traditions of Buddhism, one of the signs of the Buddha's Awakening was his ability to remember past lives, accompanied by the power of clairvoyance, which allowed him to sense and respond to the needs of others without having to be physically with others in need. A Christian example might be the visionary experiences of the resurrected, historical Jesus during moments of deep prayer, as reported by some of Jesus's disciples after the Crucifixion. These abilities, if real, go far beyond current understanding of the brain and the natural sciences. Such claims also raise anew questions about the nature of consciousness, so that any conclusions regarding this option are confronted by significant challenges of coherence.

Accordingly, it is far from clear that d'Aquili and Newberg's focus on AUB is sufficient to account for all forms of religious experience or that brain-function scans correlate with all forms of religious experience. Religious experiences are pluralistic, complex events, and it would be surprising if all could be reduced to a single kind of brain activity. Furthermore, in cognitive research thus far, no scientist has yet claimed that religious experiences have an external source, which is not what Christians who undergo these experiences report. For Christians, the source of religious experience is God, and even in Buddhist tradition, Awakening is not reduced to brain function during intense moments of meditative concentration.

Of course, the claim that God communicates directly or indirectly with human beings in some way is a central constituent of not only Christian history but Jewish and Islamic history as well. The significance of the Hebrew prophets does not lie in their personal experiences, which tend to be played down in the biblical accounts, but in their assumed ability to speak the words of God to the people of their times. Many Christians (and Jews and Muslims) have claimed, and still claim, to have received commandments from God, either as the result of prayer or unexpectedly during times of transition or crisis. Sometimes, religious experience takes the form of broad feelings of love or reassurance, or it may be more visionary in nature and include verbal communication. In all of these cases, God is experienced as the causal source of religious experience.

This is certainly the position of William Alston. He argues that religious experience is a source of sensory perception that involves biological events in the brain but is initiated by God. In the process, God relates reliable information to a person's consciousness.[35] Nancy Murphy agrees with Alston. She build's on Alston's work by incorporating the Quaker practice of discernment as a method for confirming or disconfirming the authenticity of religious experience. According to Murphy, this is the primary means for avoiding self-generating religious delusions.[36] Of course, Alston's and Murphy's work does not stress AUB experiences, which can easily be understood as achieved internally through disciplined concentration, even though such experiences are said to generate deeper comprehensions of reality.

Alston claims that no separate sensory organ is necessary to receive a revelation from God. But if we take the integration of brain and mind seriously, then presumably any revelation from God would have some effect on the brain and should be detectable by a sufficiently sophisticated brain scan. This is the thesis of Arthur Peacocke, who has argued that any experience of God is best understood as the imparting of information in a manner that invokes top-down causation.[37] According to Peacocke, God would then seem to be directly activating the relevant cognitive and emotional areas of the brain responsible for the type of religious experience in question. However, Peacocke does not address how we might know that such states of experience have been initiated by God. Still, we might presume that such an experience would have a quality of externality to it, meaning the feeling or sense that the experience was not self-produced but originated from outside of oneself.

Peacocke's account is a theoretical possibility, but it also raises questions. While it is theoretically possible that God operates in this fashion, it is also theoretically possible to stimulate God's voice or the experience of God in general in particular areas of the brain, either by experimental design or because of mental illness. Michael Persinger claims that he has done this sort of thing experimentally. He employed transcranial magnetic stimulation to stimulate neurons by magnetic pulses in a targeted brain area. He has claimed that he was able to induce religious experiences in his subjects and even in himself.[38] Assuming that Persinger's claims are valid, experimental research of this sort again raises the question, in what sense can it be determined that religious experiences are really caused by God?

At the present time, the neurosciences are incapable of answering this question because, as Philip Clayton observes, "there is something missing" in the neurosciences as now constituted.[39] No matter how complex and dynamic the neural structures of the brain may be, these structures remain physiological structures, structures that scientists must describe in third-person language. As fruitful as research into the neural correlates of consciousness may be, at best scientists can only report on a series of correlations between physical brain states and phenomenal experiences reported by subjects in first-person language. Of course, neurological third-person descriptive accounts of these correlations are empirically important, but if the resulting explanations are given exclusively in neurological terms, they will, by the nature of the case, be unable to specify what are the phenomenal *quala* that subjects experience.[40] Reductive physicalist accounts simply are not able to do justice to first-person/third-person distinctions—to what it is like to see red or listen to Beethoven or love another person or use language symbolically. The correlations of brain states observed and empirically described by neuroscientists and the first-person reports of human beings who actually experience consciousness are not the same thing;

therefore, neurological reductionism is an incoherent dead end if one wishes to understand what human beings actually experience.

Consequently, we are thrown back to a larger philosophical-theological framework in order to interpret religious experience (or any other form of experience) as reported in the first-person language of persons who have undergone these experiences. William James concluded that we should not take the validity of someone's religious experience, or our own religious experience, at face value. In the end, he believed, we must fall back on a pragmatic test of validity, articulated by both the Buddha and the historical Jesus: "You know them by their fruits." That is, we must judge religious experiences, including our own, by their effects. This is certainly valid from an ethical perspective. What that perspective may be is open to debate, but this is not the heart of the issue. What is required is a philosophy of mind grounded in neurological research, for the fact is that religious experiences are certainly real and significant for persons who experience them and for the communities they influence, even though they are not, when all is said and done, self-interpreting—another reason that a philosophical framework must be part of the methods of neurosciences investigating the physical correlates in the brain when these experiences occur. The details of such a philosophy of mind are currently an open question.

Notes

1. The "cognitive sciences" are a broad collection of disciplines united by a common philosophical perspective and research agenda that includes neuroscience, general psychology, neuropsychology, neurophysiology, cognitive psychology, artificial intelligence, linguistics, anthropology, the study of animal and human intelligence, and (highly speculative) extraterrestrial intelligence. Essentially, any scientific study of the mind, in humans or animals and perhaps in extraterrestrial beings, and its connection with the physiological structures of the brain is a "cognitive science."

2. Philip Clayton, *Mind and Emergence* (Oxford: Oxford University Press, 2004), vi.

3. Mary Hesse and Michael Arbib, *The Construction of Reality* (New York: Cambridge University Press, 1986).

4. Nancy Murphy, "Human Nature: Historical, Scientific, and Religious Issues," in *Whatever Happened to the Soul? Scientific and Theological Portraits of Human Nature*, ed. Warren S. Brown, Nancy Murphy, and H. Newton Malony (Minneapolis: Fortress Press, 1998).

5. Philip Clayton, "Theology and the Physical Sciences," in *The Modern Theologians*, ed. David F. Ford and Rachael Muers. 3rd ed. (Oxford: Blackwell Publishing, 2005), 353.

6. Philip Clayton, *Mind and Emergence: From Quantum to Consciousness* (Oxford: Oxford University Press, 2004), 106–38, 187–99.

7. Gregory R. Peterson, *Minding God: Theology and the Cognitive Sciences* (Minneapolis: Fortress Press, 2003), 42.

8. Peterson, *Minding God*, 44.

9. Gerald M. Edelman, *Neural Darwinism: The History of Neuronal Group Selection* (New York: Basic Books, 1987), cited in Peterson, *Minding God*, 42.

10. For a detailed summary of the process whereby emotions have been "mapped" in various areas of the brain, see Joseph E. LeDoux, "Emotions: A View through the Brain," in *Neuroscience and the Person: Scientific Perspectives on Divine Action*, ed. Robert John Russell, Nancy Murphy, Theo C. Meyering, and Michael A. Arbib (Vatican City: Vatican Observatory Publications, 1999), 101–17.

11. For an interesting discussion of these and other issues, see Marc Jeannerod, "Are There Limits to the Naturalization of Mental States?" in Russell, Murphy, Meyering, and Arbib, *Neuroscience and the Person*, 119–28.

12. William James, *The Variety of Religious Experience* (New York: Longmans, Green, and Company, 1912), 1–25. This is another example of the fallacy of misplaced concreteness.

13. See Michael A. Arbib, "Towards a Neuroscience of the Person," in Russell, Murphy, Meyering, and Arbib, *Neuroscience and the Person*, 77–100.

14. J. Wentzel Van Hyussteen, *The Shaping of Rationality: Towards Interdisciplinarity in Theology and Science* (Grand Rapids, MI: William B. Eerdmans Publishing, 1999).

15. Reported in *National Geographic* (March 2006): 31.

16. Ralph W. Hood Jr., Bernard Spilka, Bruce Hunsberger, and Richard Gorsuch, *The Psychology of Religion: An Empirical Approach* (New York: Guilford, 1996), 407, summarized in Peterson, *Minding God*, 106–7.

17. M. Kasamatsu and T. Harai, "An Electroencephalographic Study of the Zen Meditation (Zazen)," in *Altered States of Consciousness*, ed. C. Tart (New York: Wiley, 1969), summarized in Peterson, 107.

18. Steven T. Katz, "Language, Epistemology, and Mysticism," in *Mysticism and Philosophical Analysis*, ed. Steven T. Katz (New York: Oxford University Press, 1978), 22–74.

19. His Holiness the Fourteenth Dalai Lama, "Understanding and Transforming the Mind," in *Buddhism and Science*, ed. B. Alan Wallace (New York: Columbia University Press, 2003), 93–103.

20. David Galin, "The Concepts of 'Self,' 'Person,' and 'I' in Western Psychology and Buddhism," in Wallace, *Buddhism and Science*, 107–42.

21. Matthieu Ricard, "On the Relevance of a Contemplative Science," in Wallace, *Buddhism and Science*, 262–79.

22. James B. Ashbrook and Carol Rausch Albright, *The Humanizing Brain: Where Religion and Neuroscience Meet* (Cleveland, OH: Pilgrim, 1997), and Donald M.

MacKay, *Brains, Machines, and Persons* (Grand Rapids, MI: William B. Eerdmans Publishing, 1980).

23. MacKay, *Brains, Machines, and Persons*, 18–19.

24. Eugene d'Aquili and Andrew B. Newberg, *The Mystical Mind: Probing the Biology of Religious Experience* (Minneapolis: Fortress Press, 1999).

25. See Ted Peters, "Resurrection: The Conceptual Challenge," in *Resurrection: Theological and Scientific Assessments*, ed. Ted Peters, Robert John Russell, and Michael Welker (Grand Rapids, MI: William B. Eerdmans Publishing Company, 2002), 297–321, and Detlef B. Linke, "God Gives the Memory: Neuroscience and Resurrection," in Peters, Russell, and Welker, *Resurrection*, 185–91.

26. D'Aquili and Newberg, *The Mystical Mind*, 50–52.

27. Michael A. Sells, *Mystical Languages of Unsaying* (Chicago: University of Chicago Press, 1994), 1–13,

28. D'Aquili and Newberg, *The Mystical Mind*, 109–10, 113–14.

29. D'Aquili and Newberg, *The Mystical Mind*, 199–203.

30. See Andrew B. Newberg, Eugene d'Aquili, and Vince Rause, *Why God Won't Go Away: Brain Science and the Biology of Belief* (New York: Ballantine, 2001).

31. D'Aquili and Newberg, *The Mystical Mind*, 147–54.

32. Research cited in Peterson, *Minding God*, 112.

33. Peterson, *Minding God*, 113.

34. One of several points argued by Ian G. Barbour in "Neuroscience, Artificial Intelligence, and Human Nature: Theological and Philosophical Reflections," in Russell, Murphy, Meyering, and Arbib, *Neuroscience and the Person*, 249–80.

35. William P. Alston, *Perceiving God: The Epistemology of Religious Experience* (Ithaca, NY: Cornell University Press, 1991), ch. 1.

36. Nancy Murphy, *Theology in an Age of Scientific Reasoning* (Ithaca, NY: Cornell University Press, 1990), 152–57.

37. Arthur Peacocke, *Theology for a Scientific Age: Being and Becoming—Natural, Divine, and Human* (Minneapolis: Fortress Press, 1993), 166–83.

38. Michael A. Persinger, *Neuropsychological Bases of God Beliefs* (New York: Praeger, 1987), cited in Peterson, *Minding God*, 116.

39. Clayton, *Mind and Emergence*, 120–21.

40. Clayton, *Mind and Emergence*, 120–21.

CHAPTER SIX

❦

The Structure of
Buddhist-Christian-Science Dialogue

As noted in previous chapters, Buddhists have to this date stressed environmental ethics and psychology in their conversations about natural sciences.[1]
This assertion does not imply that Buddhists have paid no attention to
physics and other disciplines of biology. But, as in Christian theology, the focus of Buddhist interest in the natural sciences stresses those areas where traditional Buddhist teachings might be supported by current scientific views of
physical reality. In general, Buddhists interpret the natural sciences as support for the doctrine of dependent co-origination (*pratītya-samutpāda*),
which teaches that every thing and event at every moment of space-time is
co-originated because all are coconstituted by the interdependent (and interpenetrating) nexus of relationships things and events undergo from moment to moment of their existence. Furthermore, Buddhist interest in the
sciences is closely linked to the doctrines of nonself (*anatta, anātman*) and
impermanence (*anicca*). Finally, the practice of meditation has led Buddhists
to contemporary psychology and neuroscience and as a means of translating
its traditional doctrines of suffering and its causes (*duḥkha* and *taṇhā*), as well
as the meaning of Awakening (*nirvāṇa*), into a more contemporary intellectual perspective. In this regard, many Buddhists conclude that the discipline
of meditation is an empirical one similar to the empirical methodologies employed by the neurosciences. Buddhists holding this view, like the Dalai
Lama, conclude that not only do the neurosciences confirm Buddhist theories of mind and consciousness, but Buddhist concepts can also positively aid
the neurosciences in constructing a nonreductive theory of consciousness.

Accordingly, it is clear that most Buddhists do not experience or interpret the sciences as a challenge to Buddhist doctrines and practice. In fact, contemporary Buddhist writing gives the overall impression that the structure of Buddhist tradition remains untouched, either positively or negatively, by scientific inquiry. This is certainly not the case in the history of Christian encounter with the sciences.

The question now is, so what? What, if anything, would Buddhist-Christian dialogue with the natural sciences add to current Buddhist-Christian encounter? While my conclusions are very much in process, I want to begin by clarifying what I am not arguing: (1) that Buddhism is deficient because the natural sciences have not challenged Buddhist doctrines in the same way that the natural sciences have challenged Christian doctrines, (2) that Christian tradition is "truer" or "superior" to Buddhist tradition because the current scientific origin narrative can be read as a confirmation of certain Christian doctrines, or (3) that Buddhist dialogue with natural sciences should be modeled after Christian encounter with the natural sciences. Consequently, what follows should be understood as descriptive and a bit tentative.

First, it is clear that Buddhists tend to read Big Bang cosmology and other sciences as supportive of the general structure of Buddhism's worldview.[2] Buddhists seem not to have experienced any of the natural sciences as a conceptual challenge. Some Buddhist writers point to parallels between Buddhism's "nontheistic" worldview and current scientific cosmology as evidence that Buddhism is more in harmony with the sciences than Christian theism (B. Alan Wallace, Geoffrey Redmond, and Victor Mansfield). A few Buddhist writers take a stronger stance and affirm that scientific accounts of reality are proof of the superiority of Buddhism to all theistic religions (Shoyo Taniguchi). Such arguments have a familiar ring. Nineteenth- and early-twentieth-century Western scholarly interpretations of Buddhism tended to see Buddhism as "rational," "experimental," "empirical," and critical of authority beyond an individual's own experience—all treasured ideals of the Western Enlightenment. And, indeed, Buddhists have generally not thought it necessary to rethink or reformulate the fundamental doctrines that shape Buddhist thought and practice because of challenges posed by its encounter with the natural sciences.

Furthermore, as again noted in previous chapters, those Buddhists writing from Tibetan Buddhist perspectives often apply Nagarjuna's two-truths epistemology in their encounter with the sciences: scientific conclusions, models, paradigms, theories, and laws are identified as "secondary truths." The measure of the truth of scientific conclusions is "relative," "pragmatic," or "instrumental," meaning they "work," especially in the realm of technology.

But the absolute truth (i.e., "Emptying," or *śūnyāta*) is absolutely beyond "discriminating mind" based on cause-effect relations, which themselves are "empty" of "self-nature" (*svabhāva*).[3] Such notions seem contrary to Ian Barbour's notion of "critical realism," as well as the self-understanding of most working scientists, for whom scientific theories and paradigms are not "secondary truths."

Second, Buddhism's conceptual encounter with the natural sciences parallels its conceptual dialogue with Christian theology. In conceptual dialogue with Christian theology, Buddhists have not experienced the same degree of creative transformation as have Christians in their conceptual dialogue with Buddhist philosophy, perhaps because Buddhism is more worldview specific than Christian tradition. Delete or redefine any of the doctrines implicit in Buddhism's worldview—nonself, impermanence, interdependence, nontheism—and Buddhism ceases to be Buddhism. So, while a Christian theologian in dialogue with Buddhism like John Cobb can affirm in print that "[a] Christian can be a Buddhist, too"[4]—provided that one is careful to explain what this means—no Buddhist writer in conceptual dialogue with Christian theology has affirmed that a Buddhist can be a Christian, too. It seems that Buddhists have concluded that conceptual dialogue with the natural sciences as a "third party" would contribute as little to Buddhism's creative transformation as has its conceptual dialogue with Christian theology.

Nevertheless, Buddhists are as interested in the natural sciences as Christians, particularly in the practice of "socially engaged dialogue." The biological sciences have in fact proven to be particularly helpful to Buddhists and Christians in their socially engaged dialogue on environmental issues because, as noted in chapter 3, these problems cannot be addressed apart from what evolutionary theory tells us about the structure of biological processes. In fact, the major focus for Buddhists in dialogue with Christians is social engagement.[5] Including the biological and economic sciences as a third partner in socially engaged dialogue will surely empower current Buddhist and Christian cooperation in confronting issues of social and environmental justice.

Third, the neurobiological sciences might contribute to the practice of Buddhist-Christian interior dialogue. The psychological dynamics and neurophysiological processes underlying disciplines like meditation and contemplative prayer, liturgical practices, and other forms of spirituality and community might shed light on Buddhist and Christian practice traditions, both in terms of similarities and differences between the experiences such practices engender. Perhaps Buddhist-Christian interior dialogue with the neurosciences might add important new information to what is already known about Buddhist and Christian practice traditions in regard to their differences and similarities and what these differences and similarities might reveal about the nature of reality.

But is it really true that encounter with the natural sciences poses no important conceptual challenges to Buddhism's worldview or to Buddhist doctrines? Consider the following: it is a fact that, in the late twentieth century and now in the twenty-first century, the displacement of God in scientific writing is almost complete.[6] In my opinion, this is a good thing, and no scientist should place God in scientific equations. The result is both pseudoscience and incoherent theology. But watch what happens when some scientists step outside of their work as scientists and impose metaphysical conclusions relative to religious claims on the basis of their understanding and practice of science. In 1978, Edmond O. Wilson won the Pulitzer Prize for his book *On Human Nature*. Wilson's work on the social behavior of insects is widely admired as pioneering and led directly to his founding contributions to a new field, which he called "social biology," defined as the study of the biological foundations of social behavior. In the beginning of his book, Wilson clearly states what he believes to be the final displacement of God by Darwinian evolution: "If humankind evolved by Darwinian natural selection, genetic chance and environmental necessity, not God, made the species."[7] So much for the Christian doctrine of creation, scientists like Wilson declare. "No problem," Buddhists like Geoffrey Redmond believe, since Buddhist nontheism does not posit a doctrine of creation.

Again, watch what happens when scientific theory filtered through the lenses of scientific materialism is pushed to its logical conclusions. Richard Dawkins agrees with Wilson and asserts that the Darwinian universe not only displaces God, but it leaves no real place for values of genuine good or evil. "This is one of the hardest lessons for humans to learn," he writes. "We cannot admit that things might be neither good nor evil, cruel nor kind, but simply callous—indifferent to all suffering, lacking all purpose."[8] Physicist Steven Weinberg draws the same conclusion from his work in reconstructing Big Bang cosmology: "The universe is pointless."[9] First, Copernicus displaced humanity from the center of the universe. Then, materialist interpretations of Big Bang cosmology and evolutionary biology set aside God as the creator of the universe. And finally, according to this interpretation of the history of science, biochemistry and molecular biology removed all doubt that the properties of all living things can be explained in terms of the physics and chemistry of ordinary matter. Everything is made up of molecules.

For me, scientific materialist assertions about the illusory character of religious teachings, Christian or Buddhist, are summarized by the following description of the mating system of a species of monkeys, the Hanuman

Langurs, in Northern India by George C. Williams, a scientist who has made important contributions to the understanding of the complexities of natural selection.

> Their mating system is what biologists call harem polygyny: Dominant males have exclusive sexual access to a group of adult females, as long as they can keep other males away. Sooner or later, a stronger male usurps the harem and the defeated one must join the ranks of celibate outcastes. The new male shows his love for his new wives by trying to kill their unweaned infants. For each successful killing, a mother stops lactating and goes into estrous. . . . Deprived of her nursing baby, a female soon starts ovulating. She accepts the advances of her baby's murderer, and he becomes the father of her next child.
> *Do you still think that God is good?*[10]

So, there it is. If the universe is pointless and meaningless, what is the point and meaning of any religious tradition? Certainly, such conclusions are radically opposed to Christian notions of God and the whole edifice of Christian doctrine and practice. But these same views also contradict the whole edifice of Buddhism as well—if the scientific materialism of persons like Wilson, Dawkins, Weinberg, and Williams are accurate descriptions of the way things really are in this universe.

Of course, the issue for Buddhism is not the "displacement of God." Nevertheless, the notion that all living things have evolved through accidental forces of random mutation and natural selection in the struggle for existence seems to raise as many questions regarding fundamental Buddhist doctrines as it does for Christian theology. Is the teaching that, since all sentient beings are interdependent, we should experience the suffering of others as our suffering and act to relieve suffering by nonviolent expedient means based on an illusion? In a universe where the Second Law of Thermodynamics demands suffering and death as the price for life itself, does it make any sense to say we cause our own suffering by clinging to impermanence and that we can free ourselves from suffering by training ourselves not to cling to permanence? Does universal suffering have anything to do with "clinging"? If the universe really is "pointless" and "without value," can Awakening mean anything more than becoming experientially aware of universal pointlessness? If the universe is valueless, what's the value of Awakening? Are compassion and nonviolence merely fantasies? In a pointless and valueless universe, in what and for what can one reasonably hope? What is the connection between Buddhism's defining teachings and what the sciences are discovering about the physical processes of nature?

Only Buddhists can answer these questions. They are there to be answered whether or not Buddhists chose to confront them. Doing so in the context of conceptual dialogue with Christian theology and the natural sciences would, I believe, engender new forms of creative transformation in both Buddhist and Christian traditions. Exactly how remains an open question since the sciences have not, as yet, been included as dialogical partners in current Buddhist-Christian encounters. Perhaps it is time they were. As a means of starting, the structure and purpose of such a three-way dialogue is the topic of the following section. But first some preliminary observations.

The Heuristic Function of Metaphor
in Religious and Scientific Language

There are numerous options for incorporating scientific insights about physical reality into Buddhist and Christian thought and practice. These same options would deepen conceptual Buddhist-Christian dialogue. For purposes of illustration, I shall focus on quantum physics, but it must be kept in mind that there are resources within other scientific disciplines that would also illustrate the points I will argue. The governing assumption of what follows is that scientific descriptions of physical reality in all its pluralism, from quantum events to the large physical entities studied by cosmology and biology, should constrain the conclusions and practices of religious persons. This means that religious doctrines and practices should correlate as much as possible with scientific understanding of the physical process occurring in the universe at all levels, past, present, and possibly future.

For example, science informs us that there are no miracles, meaning events that are caused by an outside agency that contradict the laws of nature, which is not to say there can be no extraordinary events. Doctrines like the Resurrection or notions of omnipresent Buddhas need to be reinterpreted accordingly. It's better to go to a physician when one has cancer than to a faith healer. Likewise, literalist readings of Genesis supporting a six-day creation must be rejected given the evidence of cosmology and evolutionary biology for the age of the Earth. While I cannot speak with any authority for my Buddhist brothers and sisters on this point, there are beliefs and doctrines within the Christian tradition that are plain silly, perhaps dangerous, given what the sciences instruct us about the physical processes at play in the universe. There existed no historical Adam and Eve, original sin did not occur for the first time at a specific place in time, and the virgin birth of the historical Jesus is a literary fiction, given what we know about the biological processes of human reproduction and the fact that only two gospels, Matthew and Luke, begin their portrayals of Jesus with the virgin birth, while this tradition is ignored in the rest of the New Testament. There probably exist Buddhist teachings and practices that cannot be supported by what science tells us of physical processes as well.

The principle according to which the natural sciences constrain religious thought and practice is "critical realism," which can also be appropriated for Christian theological reflection and Buddhist philosophical reflection. Most scientists, Christian theologians, and Buddhists engaged in dialogue with the sciences are critical realists in their epistemologies: scientific, theological, and Buddhist theories and doctrines are intended to correspond to reality as it is, but they can never do so fully and are therefore capable of falsification given new evidence. Religious doctrines, like scientific conclusions, are capable of either periodical revision or rejection whenever new evidence or a better "inference to the best explanation" comes to light.

The operating principle of critical realism in the natural sciences is "inference to the best explanation" of the physical evidence. In appropriating this principle for theological and philosophical reflection and the practice of interreligious dialogue, I am in agreement with Arthur Peacocke: the natural sciences have demonstrated the unity underlying the diversity running throughout the universe as an inference to the best explanation of empirically gathered physical evidence. Translated into Christian language, the physical evidence that the universe's existence cannot but be grounded in one unifying source makes belief in God as a creator reasonable. In this sense, scientific cosmology enforces the long-held intuition of theists that God is the one underlying ground of not only all that is but also of the deep unity, interconnectedness, and wholeness of the universe.[11] Of course, Buddhists are not theists, but scientific cosmology also reinforces distinctively Buddhist inferences to the best explanation regarding the radical interdependence of all things and events as the unifying source of the universe's nondual nature.

Of course, the evidence supporting conclusions in the sciences is not identical to the evidence supporting religious conclusions. Nor are the methods of scientific investigation and theological and philosophical methodologies identical, although there are areas of similarity. Also many scientists, Christian theologians, and Buddhist philosophers do not accept the notion of critical realism, either within their own scholarly disciplines or in the practice of interreligious dialogue. I have described the conclusions of some of these scholars in chapter 2. Nevertheless, what follows will assume a critical realist stance because I think it is the most fruitful epistemological position from which religious people can dialogically engage one another and the natural sciences. Any other position, it seems to me, does little more than engender a series of scientific, Christian, and Buddhist monologues.

Before suggesting the specifics of how Buddhist and Christians might dialogically engage the natural sciences, it will be useful to reflect on the role of metaphor in the sciences, Buddhist thought, and Christian theology. According to Sally McFague, metaphors like "God is love" or "the Lord is my Shepherd" and numerous others assume a central role in Christian theological discourse.[12] Metaphors also play a central role in pointing Buddhists to the realities engendered through the practice of meditation. One immediately thinks of the chariot metaphor as a way of communicating the meaning of nonself, or the story of the frog in the *Jātaka*, or "Birth Tales," as a means of helping unenlightened seekers grasp the meaning of Awakening conceptually as a means of guiding their meditational practice. All religious traditions are replete with metaphors, as are the natural sciences (e.g., "Big Bang," "natural selection," and "struggle for existence").

But McFague also warns that whenever metaphors lose their original meaning and fruitfulness, which they invariably do when taken literally, the theology built upon them must be reconstructed, drawing upon new metaphors appropriate for a new age. The same is true in the natural sciences; machine metaphors are rapidly losing their standing in scientific discourse. Moreover, metaphors serve a cognitive function in the sciences, as well as in religion. In a religious context, metaphors illuminate such practices as prayer and meditation. Many scientists also report their own experiences of illumination through scientific metaphors. Accordingly, it seems reasonable to believe that metaphors in the natural sciences, which infuse contemporary culture, can be a source of creatively transforming Buddhist and Christian metaphorical language.

As a means of illustration, I shall draw upon examples from quantum physics, although other disciplines of the natural sciences also are a good resource for metaphors that can creatively transform both Buddhist and Christian thought and practice. But I agree with Robert John Russell that quantum physics is a primary resource for religiously meaningful metaphors in the context of contemporary culture.[13] So, while I shall draw upon certain conclusions from quantum physics in this section in order to illustrate my point about the use of metaphor, dialogue with other disciplines in the natural sciences can also serve as a resource for Buddhist and Christian creative transformation. Also, it must be understood that the citations of quantum theory I will employ do not exhaust the possibilities of appropriating quantum theory for Buddhist and Christian dialogue.

Although quantum physics and philosophers of science continue to debate the metaphysical implications, particle nonlocality, wave-particle complementarity, the measurement problem, and irreducible indeterminacy appear to run rampant at the quantum level of reality. Here, Christians might be reminded of the New Testament parable about the Kingdom of God, where divine action is at work in the universe bringing about the redemption of the world from evil and suffering, both human and naturally caused. For example, the sower of seeds on a field does not stop to direct each seed to its target, but it is guaranteed that some seeds will fall on rocky soil or among weeds, while others will fall on good soil and there take root and grow to maturity. Quantum indeterminism and chance suggest that the structures of the Kingdom of God are constrained by the random flow of ordinary processes and that hidden patterns seem to correlate, if not direct, all that happens.

In a similar way, the Buddha is said to have taught that since all sentient beings are governed by the laws of karma and samsara ("cause-effect" and "change"), the teachings of the Buddha are easily comprehended fully by some disciples, while others less karmically able may require several lifetimes to attain Awakening. According to a few texts, like the *Sukhāvatī-vyūha*, or "Discourse on the Happy Land" or the "Pure Land," a few whose negative karmic nature can never be overcome will never attain Awakening through their own efforts, even if the dharma should be transmitted to them by an Awakened monk or by the Buddha himself. Such karmically "inferior beings" require the graceful assistance of Bodhisattvas.[14] Chance and necessity seem to structure the universe even for Buddhists.

Quantum physics also provides new metaphors for surprise in nature. Nature is full of unpredictability, and we should always "expect the unexpected." In a physics lab, for example, a researcher prepares a sample containing trillions of "identical" atoms and simply waits. Quite suddenly, atoms, literally at random, begin to decay, and each "decay event" as far as any physicist can tell is without a cause. Quantum chance is not just an accident waiting to happen, the unforeseen—but in principle, predictable—intersection of two causal joints. Quantum events behave as though they are uncaused, and their surprise is of a different kind than we experience in our daily lives. Moreover, these surprise events at the quantum level radically change the history of the system involved. Atoms "decay"; they do not "reassemble" on their own. When nuclei fuse and emit light photons, they become an entirely different kind of nucleus. Particles annihilate and pair produce. Particles just don't change their properties but are transformed; the old particle perishes, a new particle is born, and the event of transformation is a surprise. Thus, quantum physics demonstrates that what Alfred North Whitehead called "perpetual perishing" is a reality from which surprising novelty arises in the foundational physical structures of nature. Deterministic causal explanations of this fact fall short of the reality being described because the scientific evidence suggests that the universe is radically changed and transformed continuously at each quantum event at every moment of space-time.

From a Christian theological perspective, this scientific fact suggests further metaphors for conceiving the Kingdom of God. John Dominic Crossan writes that Jesus's parables are structured around three themes: "advent," "reversal," and "action."[15] The kingdom appears all of a sudden, like an advent, from "nowhere," when least expected, opening up new possibilities previously unforeseen. Human response to this advent requires a reversal of the past and acting in a radically new way. Or, as Robert John Russell explains,

> the unpredictability of a quantum event is analogous to the surprise of advent and that the transformation of matter seems like the transformation of the person as we reverse our life's journey and act anew in the Spirit of God. Quantum chance seems to capture the noncognitive aspect of advent as well, the feeling of joy, fear and astonishment we experience when the *totally* unexpected truly occurs.[16]

From a Buddhist perspective, this aspect of quantum physics seems to offer powerful consonance with the Buddhist doctrine of impermanence. According to Buddhist teaching, all things and events arise out of a web of interdependent causal factors, none of which is permanent, so that the things and events that arise from these factors are also impermanent and always new. According to some strands of Mahayana philosophy, the foundation of this coarising causal network is the "emptiness" (*śūnyāta*) of substantial, independently existing, permanent self-identity through time. Or, in the words of the Heart Sutra, "form is emptiness, emptiness is form."[17] "Emptiness," or, better, "Emptying," is the source of all things and events at every moment of space-time, to translate this into the language of physics. Things and events appear from nowhere and return to nowhere in ways that cannot be predicted or determined from present realities, although present realities are part of the causal co-originating nexus from which all things and events continuously arise and disappear, in unexpected, surprising forms.

As noted in chapter 3, since Buddhism is a nontheistic religious tradition, God is not reckoned as a causal factor in Buddhist philosophy. Nevertheless, quantum physics seems to support the major conclusion of this strand of Buddhist teaching: "Nirvana *is* Samsara (Awakening *is* the phenomenal world of change and becoming) since all things originate in 'Emptying' and return to Emptying," like lotus flowers floating on a pond whose roots are in nondifferentiated mud, to which the flower eventually returns. No two lotus flowers, like no two things or events, are identical or permanent, yet Emptying (like mud in a pond) takes all things and events into itself, while simultaneously generating new patterns of things and events in a process without beginning or end. Realizing Emptying through the process of meditation, one attains the wisdom of Awakening that is *nirvāṇa*, a primary symbol of which is Indra's jeweled net.[18]

In the heavenly abode of Indra, the king of the gods, there is hung a wonderful net that stretches out in all directions. The net's clever weaver has strung a single jewel in each eye, and since the net is infinite in dimension, the jewels are infinite in number. If we look carefully at a single jewel, we discover that its polished surface reflects every other jewel. Not only that, each of the jewels we are looking at simultaneously reflects all the other jewels, so that there is an infinite reflecting process. Indra's jeweled net is a primary metaphor in Mahayana Buddhism used to characterize the natural order as an infinitely repeating series of interrelationships simultaneously occurring in all particular entities. It illustrates, in other words, the doctrine of dependent co-origination. Quantum physics seems to support this aspect of Buddhist tradition quite well.

Consonance with quantum physics does not "prove" that the central metaphors of either Buddhism or Christianity correspond to the way reality actually is in regard to either the physical details of the universe or the wider experiential details of distinctively Buddhist or Christian religious doctrine and practice. No religious tradition is "scientific." There are a number of reasons for this judgment. Science deals with very narrow bands of experience of physical processes. To do so requires intentionally ignoring wider bodies of experience—ethical, religious, political, aesthetic—in the application of scientific methods of research. Biologist Francisco Ayala refers to this methodological practice as "methodological naturalism."[19] But methodological naturalism does not mean that working scientists do not have ethical, religious, political, or aesthetic experiences and beliefs. These experiences, however, should never be intentionally employed as an element of scientific investigation. A scientist can be a religious person, or not, but religious ideas and practices can have no application in scientific theory and experimentation. Methodological naturalism is the source of science's great explanatory power, as well as of its universalism, but at a price. Science transcends culture and political and religious differences because the narrowness of its focus makes it incompetent in these areas of human experience.

And yet, science can and does inform, as it constrains, ethical, religious, political, and aesthetic experience and conclusions. Many working scientists are deeply ethical, as well as socially and political engaged, and persons of deep religious commitment. Many scientists, like Albert Einstein, who participated in no religious tradition, as well as physicists like John Polkinghorne and Ian Barbour and biologists like Arthur Peacocke, all trained in the art of theological reflection, experience the beauty and intelligibility of the universe as its deepest mystery, akin to what mystics in all religious traditions describe as beyond the categories of thought and conceptuality. Likewise, many religious persons experience a deepening of faith the more they know about the physical universe and the methods of working scientists that unravel its structures and make them intelligible. But science qua science is incapable of theological and philosophical reflection, just as theological and philosophical reflection qua theological and philosophical reflection are incapable of scientific investigation.

But the conversation between science and religion should not be understood as a one-way monologue. If science did not have much to gain from dialogue with religion, no religious dialogue with the natural sciences would be possible. A dialogue is a two-way conversation, where participants and experts in different disciplines and religious traditions have space to engage one another for their mutual creative transformation. Since I have used this term throughout this book, it is time to clarify what I mean.

Creative transformation is a technical term employed by process theology and is an interpretation of Whitehead's understanding of creativity as metaphysically ultimate. My philosophical orientation is process philosophy. Thus, according to Whitehead,

> Creativity is the universal of universals characterizing ultimate matters of fact. It is that ultimate principle by which the many, which are the universe disjunctively, become the one actual occasion, which is the universe conjunctively. It lies in the nature of things that the many enter into complex unity.[20]

Essentially, creative transformation is a process of growth and novelty and is the essence of life itself. Growth is not achieved by merely adding together elements in the given world in different combinations, as if one were mixing a salad. It requires the transformation of those elements through the introduction of novelty. Consequently, creative transformation is a process that alters the nature of these elements without suppressing or destroying them. Because creativity is part of Whitehead's categorical scheme through which he appropriates Einstein's theories of special and general relativity, quantum physics, and evolutionary biology, creativity does not have for him an existence or actuality apart from concrete actual occasions of experience. That is, creativity has no existence in itself but is found only in actual instances of the "many becoming one and increased by one." In this sense, creativity is very similar to the Buddhist doctrine of dependent coarising.

For Christian tradition, the source of novelty is the Logos, whose incarnation is the historical Jesus as the Christ. Where Christ is effectively present, there is creative transformation.[21] For Buddhists, wherever the dharma is present, there is creative transformation. Mutual creative transformation is the goal of dialogue, particularly Buddhist-Christian dialogue. It occurs when Buddhists and Christians engage one another in nonmonological conversation, learn from one another, mutually appropriate what can be appropriated, and thereby deepen their own particular religious understanding, faith, and practice in a process of mutual renewal.[22]

The process of mutual creative transformation implies that Buddhists and Christians have truthful insights about the structure of existence that may not be fully evident in either Buddhist or Christian understanding about the nature of reality that can be mutually shared. Without this assumption, conversation between Buddhists and Christians can only be a monologue. It is also quite clear that the natural sciences have much to offer Buddhists and Christians as a source of creative transformation in both traditions. So far, however, I have described this as a one-way conversation, where science rightly assumes the role of teacher of Buddhist and Christian students in matters of physical fact and theory about the universe. However, if this is the only way that the sciences can engage Buddhism and Christianity, the conversation can only be another form of monologue where science has nothing to gain from the conversation. So, the question is whether it is possible for the natural sciences to be creatively transformed by dialogue with Buddhism and Christianity. This can only occur if Buddhism and Christianity have important contributions to make to the self-understanding of working scientists so that the sciences have something positive to gain from the conversation. How the natural sciences might be creatively transformed through dialogue with Buddhist and Christian tradition is the topic of the following section.

Possible Buddhist-Christian
Contributions to the Natural Sciences

Mikael Stenmark argues that there are four ways in which "religious worldviews" could and should make substantial contributions to the development of the natural sciences: (1) shaping the "problem-stating phase" of science, (2) shaping the "developmental phase" of science, (3) shaping the "justification phase" of science, and (4) shaping the "application phase" of science.[23]

I shall argue that Buddhist-Christian conceptual dialogue with the natural sciences might contribute to the problem-stating phase, the developmental phase, and the justification phase, while socially engaged dialogue might contribute to the application phase of the sciences. The question is in what sense this conclusion is appropriate, so that the inner integrity of the natural sciences is not limited by unnecessary ideologically constructed religious views not appropriate to the specifics of scientific research and conclusion formation. Stenmark is a philosopher of religion writing in general about what he conceives the proper interaction between science and "religious worldviews" to be. But his analysis provides a good starting framework for considering the more specific contributions that Buddhism and Christianity might or might not make to the natural sciences.

The Problem-Stating Phase of Science

In common with scholars in other disciplines, scientists must first decide what is worth studying. The issues here are how scientists want to spend their time, their energy, and their own or other people's economic resources on their various research projects. Imre Lakatos writes that the sciences ought to be autonomous in the sense that the direction of research should proceed undisturbed and not be determined by any ideological or religious interests. He argues that the wider society beyond the scientific community should never be allowed to *determine* the choice of scientific problems and research areas.[24] Lakatos's concern is that integrity of science is always threatened by political interests and often by religious interests.

This seems to be a matter of obvious fact and one with which religious persons should concur. People and groups in power—governments, corporations, religious institutions—often decide the kind of research agendas scientists should pursue and which agendas should be ignored. A contemporary American example of this is the denial of federal funding for stem cell research by the Republican majority in the U.S. Congress and President George W. Bush's administration, motivated by the desire to gain political advantage with conservative evangelical and fundamentalist Christian organizations. In cases like this, scientists often have to make the difficult choice between doing their research under these conditions and not doing it at all. Science has indeed become heavily politicized and often religiously and ideologically partisan. Yet, the issue is not only "big science." There are certain areas that interest rich but not poor people, white people but not people of color, men but not women, Christians but not non-Christians or secularists, liberals but not conservatives, and this will sometimes determine what scientists decide not to work on or choose not to investigate. For instance, Richard Dawkins has stated in print that his choice of research interests in biology derives from his wish to be an "intellectually fulfilled atheist," which he thinks Charles Darwin made possible, and his intention to employ his research to defend atheism against all forms of theism.[25]

One conclusion that can be reasonably drawn at this juncture is that the autonomy of science or any other scholarly discipline partially overlaps with the issue of whether religious or political ideology should shape it. For it is a fact that even if scientists are free to shape the sciences by pursuing any research area or questions in any way they chose, science still remains religiously and ideologically partisan because most scientists adhere, whether or not they are aware of it, to one worldview or another, one religious tradition or another (or no religious tradition), one political stance or another, one economic philosophy or another.

Still, it's one thing for working scientists who are committed to, say, Buddhism, Christianity, Islam, or atheistic naturalism to be influenced by their worldview commitments in the selection of questions and research agendas. But it is quite another thing when religious people, politicians, or non–scientifically trained people in general are allowed to determine ideologically the agenda for scientific research. So, the question is, should worldview influence on science be eliminated from the practice of science? The answer is that this is not possible. Scientific development may even at times benefit from such influence because some topics, some research programs, some things that require explanation, might not be noticed by working scientists because of the particular worldview uncritically influencing their work. Therefore, it seems quite reasonable to affirm religious or philosophical motives to guide the kind of research scientists pursue, particularly when scientists themselves set their research agendas. The real question is, what kinds of religious assumptions, worldviews, or ideologies are influencing scientific research?

Here, Buddhist-Christian conceptual dialogue with the natural sciences might aid in clarifying uncritically recognized religious, philosophical, or ideological assumptions at work in specific scientific agendas at the problem stating, developmental, and justification phases of scientific research. Buddhist-Christian conceptual dialogue might thereby engender more critical self-awareness of ideological interpretations of science that cannot be coherently supported by scientific methods or the objects of scientific research. More specifically, the reductionisms of scientific materialism might not so easily be assumed by many working scientists if they were more critically aware of reductionist presuppositions that explain by explaining away whole areas of experience—music, beauty, ethical sensitivity, longings for justice, or experiences of love, self-consciousness, and religious experience—as the motions of physical events. Buddhist-Christian conceptual dialogue would serve the sciences well as a reminder that its methods and conclusions are only relevant to a small area of physical reality. Important as these areas are, they do not constitute the totality of the structure of existence.

At the same time, however, neither Buddhist nor Christian doctrines, teachings, or practices have any authority in themselves for setting research agendas or deciding scientific questions. Furthermore, not all forms of Buddhism or Christianity are able to engage the sciences dialogically because they are ideologically antiscience. Examples abound: forms of popular Buddhism that stress karmic causes of physical and mental illness and the need for changing the cause-effect relations governing one's life in order to be cured of these illnesses are not conducive to dialogue with the sciences; Christian forms of fundamentalism, the intelligent design movement, or apocalyptic forms of Christian theology are not conducive to dialogue with the natural sciences, let alone dialogue with non-Christian religious traditions.

But "mainline" forms of Buddhism and Christianity are quite capable of making meaningful contributions to the practice of science through dialogue. For instance, Buddhist tradition affirms that all things and events at every moment of space-time are interdependently related, so that no thing or event is ever separated from any other thing or event. One conclusion Buddhists draw from the doctrine of interdependence is that because we are so interdependently linked, the suffering of any sentient being is the suffering of all sentient beings. Consequently, Buddhists can reasonably ask scientists to refrain from conducting any kind of research that could be harmful to human and nonhuman life (the problem-stating phase). Similarly, Buddhist interest in ecology, also motivated by universal compassion, might inspire more scientific research into the biological structures that support Buddhist views on the environment (the application and justification phases).[26]

The Christian doctrine of the incarnation of the Logos in the historical Jesus as the Christ, particularly as read through the filter of the prologue to the Gospel of John, can also be read as a ringing declaration of the interdependence of all things as a creative action of God, both in the past origins of the universe and in God's continuing creative activity in the universe. Christians inspired by this interpretation of the incarnation and the doctrine of creation might be also inspired to ask scientists to refrain from research that is harmful to life. This, in turn, can promote scientific research as a means to promote economic, social, and gender justice for human beings, ecological justice for both human beings and other sentient beings, and the creation of technology that decreases the violence persons impose on one other and on the environment (the problem stating, developmental, justifi-cation, and application phases). Another important example is Christian en-couragement of stem cell research, of which there are numerous examples not often noted in American news media.[27]

The Developmental Phase of Science

A major question in the general science-religion dialogue is whether reli-gious or philosophical commitments should influence the development of science. As scientists chose their areas of research, they try to find methods suitable for solving problems as they develop hypotheses that provide ade-quate explanation of whatever physical phenomena are under investigation. Then, these hypotheses are tested against what the scientific community regards as evidence. If there is not sufficient evidence, scientists try to find other conclusions established on better evidence. Moreover, scientists invent concepts in order to express their hypotheses and the evidence and to clas-sify evidence into different categories. They present their findings in papers and journals and at public conferences and try to take into account criticism from the wider scientific community.

Historically, religious or philosophical considerations have in fact played a role in the developmental phase of science. For example, the "man-the-hunter" hypothesis in paleoanthropology, according to feminist analysis, cul-turally embodied a sexist assumption about human nature that uncritically led paleoanthropologists to think only in terms of male activity, coupled with a reluctance to conclude that early Homo sapiens engaged in any activity other than hunting. This sexist view was certainly an ideological constraint on their capacity to develop and evaluate hypotheses explaining the evolu-tion of the human species and tool making. The most reasonable explana-tion for this particular hypothesis is that its supporters were deeply influ-enced, perhaps unconsciously, by the gender stereotypes they projected into the past. On the other hand, a possible explanation for the "woman-the-gatherer" hypothesis might be the rise of the women's movement in the 1970s, with its insistence on making women "visible." In this context, it is evident that scientists were rightly forced to begin asking questions about the role of women in cultural evolution. "Woman-the-gatherer" is a hypothesis that expressed the feminist movement's progressive political values and ideals projected onto the past, although it is also certainly more than an ide-ological assumption because of the historical evidence that supports it.

Three points require clarification. First, scientific research might be moti-vated by religious, philosophical, or political assumptions and still produce re-liable knowledge and theoretical constructions. Religious and philosophical considerations do not necessarily entail injecting debilitating bias into science. This does not mean that a scientist's religious or philosophical commitments never distort conclusions in unjustifiable ways not reflective of scientific method. It's very difficult to justify the conclusions of "scientific creationism" or the intelligent design movement's conclusion regarding evolutionary theory as "scientific." Nor are the specific theological conclusions of these movements particularly coherent. Consequently, it is important to avoid the fallacy of guilt by association when considering the developmental phase of science and the possibilities of religious dialogue with the sciences.

Second, it is neither possible nor necessary to restrict the way scientists arrive at their hypotheses. If a particular scientist arrives at a hypothesis by reading the Bible, a Buddhist text, the Qur'an, or Marx's *Das Capital* or is inspired by feminist thought rather than "pure curiosity" (whatever this might mean) about how nature works, it probably does not matter all that much—from a scientific point of view—as long as coherent and testable hypotheses are produced, supported by proper evidence that explains physical phenomena in an illuminating and fruitful way. Religious worldviews, like other worldviews and ideologies, can then be allowed to play a *heuristic role* in constructing hypotheses within particular scientific disciplines. There is every reason to think that Buddhist-Christian dialogue with the sciences might be of service in this phase of scientific work.

Even so, worldview-partisan science is problematic in one sense. Whenever science is dominated by a particular group of people (men, women, Christians, Buddhists, socialists, political liberals, or conservatives), it is often impossible to develop hypotheses that explain the data better than the officially supported hypotheses guiding the majority of scientists in control of the discipline. This is also a fact of reality in other disciplines, including theology and philosophy. I remember as a teaching associate at the University of California, Santa Barbara, that it was impossible for undergraduate or graduate students to enroll in courses in metaphysics, ancient philosophy, or medieval philosophy in the Philosophy Department because no courses in these areas were offered by the philosophy faculty. All of my philosophy colleagues were trained in analytical philosophy and did not think other areas of philosophy were important. But courses in metaphysics, ethics, and the history of philosophy were offered by the Religious Studies Department, so students interested in these areas were instructed by religious studies faculty. A good way to avoid a similar situation in the natural sciences is to make sure that the scientific community remains philosophically and religiously pluralistic, meaning as open as possible to working scientists representing different religious and philosophical perspectives. Science qua science is not about evangelizing persons into a particular world-view, religious tradition, or philosophical perspective. In this regard, Christian and Buddhist contributions might entail encouraging scientists to remain open to religious and philosophical pluralism as a means of not confusing scientific theory with ideology.

The Application Phase of Science
Questions about the application phase of science have to do with whether it is appropriate to promote the interests of particular ethnic groups, social classes, genders, or religion. Scientific knowledge and theory is now to a large extent guided by its technological application in the wider society beyond the university and other scientific research institutions, which up to now have been the traditional institutions of knowledge production and theoretical construction in all academic fields. In new research fields in the natural sciences, for example biotechnology, the boundaries between university and industrial/military research have now almost disappeared. In light of this fact, it is particularly difficult to affirm the ideal of a worldview-neutral science. Hence, the view that the natural sciences can be completely worldview neutral is an illusion.

The main difference between a science open to religious values and ideas and a secular science is not merely that, with the former, the metaphysical presuppositions of science are rooted in a religious worldview while with the latter they are not, but that religious considerations direct the applications of scientific research at the technological, practical levels of application. It may be reasonably argued that Buddhist-Christian conceptual and socially engaged dialogue with the sciences is particularly relevant at this stage. Yet, most scientists, even those who are Christians or Buddhists, view science itself as neutral with respect to philosophy and religion. So, for example, while it is true that many scientists who are Christian understand standard Big Bang cosmology as evidence supporting their belief in God and many Buddhists accept the findings of neuroscience as support for Buddhist doctrines of mental causation and the practice of meditation, it is also true that most scientists follow a secularist-naturalist path in their research, even if they are participants in a religious tradition. It is the belief that science *must* remain ideologically neutral that leads to the view that science as such has no ethical or social responsibility. As Lakatos writes,

> In my view, science, as such, has no social responsibility. In my view it is society that has responsibility—that of maintaining the apolitical, detached scientific tradition and allowing science to search for truth in the way determined purely

by its inner life. Of course, scientists, as citizens, have responsibility, like all other citizens, to see that science is *applied* to the right social and political ends. This is a different, independent question.[28]

Or, as Edward Teller writes,

The scientist's responsibility is to find out what he can about nature. It is his responsibility to use new knowledge to extend man's power over nature. . . . When the scientist has learned what he can learn and when he has built what he is able to build, his work is not yet done. He must also explain in clear, simple, and understandable terms what he has found and what he has constructed. And there his responsibility ends. The decision on how to use the results of science are not his. The right and duty to make decisions belongs to the people.[29]

Accordingly, Lakatos and Teller argue, the ends to which scientific research are applied should be determined by the people in a democratic society. Within the framework of democracy—a political ideology, be it noted—ordinary persons are equally able to apply the discoveries and technological applications of science for whatever vision of a meaningful human life they endorse, be this feminist, Christian, Buddhist, Marxist, or secularist. But scientists qua scientists must remain neutral to ethical, political, and religious values.

The problem with this argument is that scientific knowledge is to a large degree generated in the context of its technological applications. The history of science clearly demonstrates that it is not possible to exclude technological application entirely from "pure" scientific research proper. Today, much, but of course not all, scientific research is done in the context of its technological application. Here, the emphasis is on "useful answers" to the ever-increasing, practical, social, economic, environmental, medical, and economic problems of society as a whole. The meaning of "useful answers" depends, however, on the ideology of funding institutions, the political and economic philosophy of government leaders and bureaucrats, the economic goals of corporations, and the application of technology in times of war. In this situation, it is quite meaningful to conclude that conceptual and socially engaged dialogue with Buddhism and Christianity might be a meaningful source for shaping the technological applications of science.

It also seems reasonable to conclude that scientists ought not carry out their research without first considering ethical questions engendered by their work. How will the results of a research program be used technologically and who or what group will direct its use? If it is clear that technological applications of science will violate widely accepted ethical assumptions and practices, scientists should be encouraged to refuse to carry out their research without adequate ethical considerations. That is, science should be guided by ethical principles, which of course are not free-floating principles but rather rooted in powerful religious experiences and sensibilities. Buddhist and Christian notions of nonviolence, interdependence, and justice might make important contributions to working scientists as they confront the ethical, political, and economic consequences of their work.

The Justification Phase of Science

The justification phase refers to the processes by which scientists working on particular research projects try to persuade the rest of the scientific community to accept their conclusions, explanations, theories, concepts, and methods. A similar "justification phase" occurs in Christian theological reflection and missionology and in Buddhist thought and the history of Buddhist transmission throughout the world. In relation to science, the question is, can Buddhist or Christian tradition make contributions to the natural sciences relative to this aspect of scientific work? One could also ask if the sciences have anything to contribute to the justification phase of Christianity or Buddhism relative to Christian or Buddhist missions. That science could be open to Buddhist or Christian worldviews is certainly a possibility. An equal possibility is that Christianity and Buddhism can and should be open to scientific understandings of physical reality. Science can also reasonably expect its practitioners to be methodologically neutral regarding any religious or philosophical tradition. Likewise, Christian tradition is not locked into a specific methodology or worldview, other than monotheism, and is less worldview dependent than traditional Buddhist thought and practice. Given this, the question is whether Buddhism and Christianity can, in their dialogue with the sciences, creatively influence the sciences at this phase of scientific work.

Two things require consideration. First, science should in fact be religiously and philosophically neutral in all phases of science in the sense that it ought not *presuppose* the truth of any particular religious tradition or philosophical worldview, such as metaphysical materialism, as necessary for the practice of science. Neither Christian "creation science" nor "intelligent design" nor the materialist worldview of biologists such as E. O. Wilson should influence the work of scientists at any phase of scientific investigation. Of course, the "naturalism" assumed by most scientists is a philosophical worldview, but this is epistemologically appropriate as a methodological principle presupposed by scientists so long as it does not evolve into metaphysical reductionism.

In principle, scientists are concerned with very limited aspects of the totality of experience. Naturalism "works" in regard to physical facts; it does not "work" coherently when consideration is given to wider bodies of experience considered by ethics, aesthetics, economics, theology, or philosophy. The methodological reductionism supported by scientific naturalism—reducing all physical phenomena to the casual relations between physical particles— is incoherent when applied to wider bodies of experience. Thus, it is perfectly coherent to explain how the motion of air molecules bouncing off my eardrums sends electrical impulses through synaptic cells to appropriate areas of my brain, allowing me to hear music. But this naturalist explanation does not explain why I love classical music, jazz piano, and Gregorian chant. The power of science rests in ignoring most experience as it concentrates on very narrow bands of reality.

So, theories should be adopted or rejected by the scientific community only in light of evidence that involves empirical data gathered experimentally for the most part, the most coherent explanation of the data, and the most ex- planatory power. Also, scientific conclusions are in principle falsifiable and ca- pable of revision and rejection, as are the theological and philosophical con- clusions of Buddhism and Christianity. But Christianity and Buddhism can have nothing to offer the sciences in this regard. Religious considerations are always illegitimate factors when deciding between scientific theories.

Postscript

The natural sciences inspire great reverence, wonder, and awe for most sci- entists and many religious persons throughout the world's religious traditions. This is so because the sciences provide a continual stream of remarkable in- sights into the nature of physical reality across a wide range of domains. In doing so, the sciences change both our world and our worldviews, and, in the process, our understanding of ourselves. Here lies the source of the many conceptual challenges to all religious traditions and systems of practice. As the pace of scientific discovery and innovation exponentially increases, there arises an urgent cultural need to reflect thoughtfully and critically on these changes and challenges in a constructive dialogue involving the world's reli- gious traditions, including, of course, Buddhism and Christianity. One of the greatest challenges in the twenty-first century will be to bridge the compart- mentalization of knowledge currently institutionalized in modern universi- ties. This will entail engaging in an integrative dialogue among all the sci- ences, humanities, and the world's religious traditions.

The purpose of interdisciplinary and interreligious dialogue is mutual cre- ative transformation. For mutual creative transformation to occur within Buddhist-Christian dialogue with the natural sciences, integrative dialogue will need to honor the complex details of each of the natural sciences and Buddhist and Christian traditions. Of course, contradictory views regarding the nature of reality need to be honestly recognized. But it must also be recognized that upon closer critical reflection, what looks like contradictions may be revealed to be different ways of understanding the same reality. Ultimately, no truths can be contradictory if they are really true, provided we do not lock ourselves up within a particular intellectual discipline or religious perspective, which runs the risk of confusing ideology for truth. Furthermore, we must not shrink from the task of building exploratory networks for considering issues of broad social, economic, and environmental significance for the lives of human beings and other beings with whom we share this planet. This will require that dialogue not be limited to professional academics or religious leaders but widened to include persons sitting in the pews of churches and synagogues or on mats in temples or on prayer rugs in mosques, as well as persons reading about scientific discoveries in the Tuesday Science Section of the *New York Times* at the breakfast table.

Exactly how such an integrative interreligious dialogue with the natural sciences should be structured is, of course, an open question, but there are contemporary precedents upon which to draw. Since 1980, the Society for Buddhist-Christian Studies has been an important model for the practice of integrative interreligious dialogue. Currently, the Lutheran Theological Seminary in Chicago is now one of the important centers of Islamic-Christian encounter in the United States. There also exist organizations focusing on Hindu-Christian and Confucian-Christian dialogue in the United States and in Europe. But little effort has been made to incorporate the natural sciences systematically as a third partner into these expressions of interreligious dialogue. And so, both the challenges and the opportunities for creative transformation that conversation with the sciences fosters are, for the most part, ignored.

Yet, there are movements afoot within the natural sciences that seek to build dialogical bridges with the world's religious traditions. One immediately thinks of the Templeton Foundation's Metanexus Institute and the Center for Theology and the Natural Sciences in Berkeley, California, as well as the Center for Process Studies in Claremont, California. Many such groups now exist throughout North America and Europe. Yet, these associations are mostly focused on dialogue with Christian theology, even though there have been efforts to include Buddhist, Jewish, and Islamic scholars in the conversation with the disciplines of science. More effort needs to be made toward expanding these scientific dialogues with religion to include all of the world's religions.

Accordingly, the final conclusion of this book is one that is still in process. This conclusion stems from my participation within the Lutheran expression of Christian faith and my participation in Buddhist-Christian dialogue: the two most important theological tasks confronting thinking Christians are (1) dialogue with the world's religious traditions and (2) dialogue with the natural sciences. Even though I have come to this conclusion engaged in dialogue with Buddhists, I suspect it applies to thinking religious persons in all religious traditions. Both tasks are interdependent and demand intentionally bringing the natural sciences into interreligious dialogue as a third partner. This has not as yet happened in any systematic fashion in any specific interreligious dialogue, including contemporary Buddhist-Christian dialogue. It's time to start.

Notes

1. See, for example, Mary Evelyn Tucker and Duncan Ryukan Williams, eds., *Buddhism and Ecology* (Cambridge, MA: Harvard University, 1997), and three essays in J. Baird Callicott and Roger T. Ames, eds., *Nature in Asian Traditions of Thought* (Albany: State University of New York, 1989): Francis Cook, "The Jeweled Net of Indra" (213–30), Kenneth K. Inada, "Environmental Problems" (231–46), and David J. Kaluphana, "Toward a Middle Path of Survival" (247–58).

2. In previous chapters of this book, I have described aspects of Buddhist reflection on the usefulness of evolutionary and psychological theory as these relate to the doctrine of impermanence and the practice of meditation. Many Buddhists conclude that these sciences are particularly useful in understanding environmental issues, as well as enhancing the practice of meditation through the development of a coherent theory of consciousness free from the "objectivist bias of Western psychology."

3. Frederick J. Streng, *Emptiness: A Study in Religious Meaning* (Nashville: Abingdon Press, 1967), chs. 2–3.

4. John B. Cobb Jr., "Can a Christian Be a Buddhist, Too?" *Japanese Religions* 10 (1979): 1–20.

5. Cf. Tucker and Williams, *Buddhism and Ecology*; Christopher S. Queen and Sallie B. King, eds., *Engaged Buddhism: Buddhist Liberation Movements in Asia* (New York: State University of New York, 1996); and Christopher S. Queen, ed., *Engaged Buddhism in the West* (Boston: Wisdom Publications, 2000).

6. See Kenneth R. Miller, *Finding Darwin's God: A Scientist's Search for Common Ground between God and Evolution* (New York: Cliff Street Books, 1999), 15.

7. E. O. Wilson, *On Human Nature* (Cambridge, MA: Harvard University Press, 1978), 1.

8. Richard Dawkins, *River out of Eden* (New York: Harper Collins, 1995), 95–96.

9. Steven Weinberg, *The First Three Minutes* (New York: Basic Books, 1988), 150–55.

10. George C. Williams, *The Pony Fish's Glow* (New York: Harper Collins, 1997), 156–57, cited in Miller, *Finding Darwin's God*, 16.

11. Arthur Peacocke, *Theology for a Scientific Age* (Minneapolis: Fortress Press, 1993), 101–2.

12. Sallie McFague, *Metaphorical Theology: Models of God in Religious Language* (Philadelphia: Fortress Press, 1982), and *Models of God: Theology for an Ecological, Nuclear Age* (Minneapolis: Fortress Press, 1987).

13. See chapters 3 through 5. Also see Robert John Russell, "Quantum Physics in Theological Perspective," in *Physics, Philosophy, and Theology: A Common Quest for Understanding*, ed. Robert John Russell, Willian R. Stoeger, and George V. Coyne (Notre Dame, IN: University of Notre Dame Press, 1988), 355–69.

14. See Bunno Kato, trans., *Myho-Renge-Kyo: The Sutra of the Lotus Flower of the Wonderful Law* (Tokyo: Kosei Publishing Company, 1971), ch. 15.

15. John Dominic Crossan, *In Parables: The Challenge of the Historical Jesus* (New York: Harper and Row: 1973), 33 ff, also referenced in Russell, "Quantum Physics in Theological Perspective," 356.

16. Russell, "Quantum Physics in Theological Perspective," 356.

17. See Donald S. Lopez Jr., *The Heart Sutra Explained: Indian and Tibetan Commentaries* (Albany: State University of New York Press, 1988), for a detailed analysis of this Buddhist text.

18. See Francis H. Cook, "The Jeweled Net of Indra," in Callicott and Ames, *Nature in Asian Traditions of Thought*, 213–29.

19. Francisco J. Ayala, *Darwin and Intelligent Design* (Minneapolis: Fortress Press, 2006), 101.

20. Alfred North Whitehead, *Process and Reality: Corrected Edition*, ed. David Ray Griffin and Donald W. Sherburne (New York: The Free Press, 1978), 21.

21. See John B. Cobb Jr. and David Ray Griffin, *Process Theology: An Introductory Exposition* (Philadelphia: Westminster Press, 1976), 100–101.

22. See my essay "Interfaith Dialogue as a Source of Buddhist-Christian Creative Transformation, " in *Buddhist-Christian Dialogue: Mutual Renewal and Transformation*, ed. Paul O. Ingram and Frederick J. Streng (Honolulu: University of Hawaii Press, 1986), 77–94.

23. Mikael Stenmark, *How to Relate Science and Religion* (Grand Rapids, MI: William B. Eerdmans Publishing Company, 2004), 216.

24. Imre Lakatos, *Mathematics, Science, and Epistemology*, vol. 2. of *Philosophical Papers*, ed. John Worrall and Gregory Currie (Cambridge: Cambridge University Press, 1978), 258.

25. Richard Dawkins, *The Blind Watchmaker* (New York: W. W. Norton, 1986), 6.

26. Alan Sponberg, "Green Buddhism and the Hierarchy of Compassion," in *Buddhism and Ecology*, ed. Mary Evelyn Tucker and Duncan Ryukan Williams (Cambridge, MA: Harvard University Press, 1997), 351–76.

27. For one of the most convincing theological arguments supporting stem cell research, see Ted Peters, *Science, Theology, and Ethics* (Burlington, VT: Ashgate Publishing, 2003), ch. 9.

28. Lakatos, *Mathematics, Science, and Epistemology*, 258, italics in the original.

29. Edward Teller, *The Reluctant Revolutionary* (Columbia, MO: University of Missouri Press, 1960), 2–21, cited in Stenmark, *How to Relate Science and Religion*, 226.

Selected Bibliography

Alston, William P. *Perceiving God: The Epistemology of Religious Experience.* Ithaca, NY: Cornell University Press, 1991.

Arbib, Michael A. "Towards a Neuroscience of the Person." In *Neuroscience and the Person: Scientific Perspectives on Divine Action,* ed. Robert John Russell, Nancy Murphy, Theo C. Meyering, and Michael A. Arbib, 77–100. Vatican City: Vatican Observatory Publications, 1999.

Ashbrook, James B., and Albright, Carol Rausch. *The Humanizing Brain: Where Religion and Neuroscience Meet.* Cleveland, OH: Pilgrim, 1997.

Augustine. *Confessions.* Oxford: Oxford University Press, 1991.

Ayala, Francisco J. *Darwin and Intelligent Design.* Minneapolis: Fortress Press, 2006.

———. "The Structure of Evolutionary Theory: On Stephen Jay Gould's Monumental Masterpiece." *Theology and Science* 3 (March 2005): 103–17.

Barbour, Ian G. "Evolution and Process Thought." *Theology and Science* 3 (July 2005): 160–78.

———. *Religion and Science: Historical and Contemporary Issues.* San Francisco: Harper San Francisco, 1997.

———. *Issues in Science and Religion.* New York: Harper Torchbooks, 1966.

———. "Neuroscience, Artificial Intelligence, and Human Nature: Theological and Philosophical Reflections." In *Neuroscience and the Person: Scientific Perspectives on Divine Action,* ed. Robert John Russell, Nancy Murphy, Theo C. Meyering, and Michael A. Arbib, 249–80. Vatican City: Vatican Observatory Publications, 1999.

———. *Religion and Science.* San Francisco: Harper San Francisco, 1997.

Barth, Karl. *Dogmatics in Outline.* New York: Harper and Row, 1949.

Behe, Michael J. *Darwin's Black Box: The Biochemical Challenge to Evolution.* New York: Free Press, 1996.

Berg, Christian. "Barbour's Way(s) of Relating Science and Religion." In *Fifty Years in Science and Religion: Ian G. Barbour and His Legacy*, ed. Robert John Russell, 61–76. Burlington, VT: Ashgate Publishing, 2004.

Birch, Charles, and Cobb, John B., Jr. *The Liberation of Life*. Cambridge: Cambridge University Press, 1981.

Brooke, John Hedley. *Science and Religion: Some Historical Perspectives*. Cambridge: Cambridge University Press, 1991.

Brown, Warren S., Murphy, Nancy, and Malony, H. Newton, eds. *Whatever Happened to the Soul? Scientific and Theological Portraits of Human Nature*. Minneapolis: Fortress Press, 1998.

Burton, Naomi, Hart, Patrick, and Laughlin, James, eds., *The Asian Journal of Thomas Merton*. New York: New Directions Publishing Corporation, 1973.

Cabezón, José Ignacio. "Buddhism and Science: On the Nature of the Dialogue." In *Buddhism and Science: Breaking New Ground*, ed. B. Allan Wallace, 35–68. New York: Columbia University Press, 2003.

Callicott, J. Baird, and Ames, Roger T., eds. *Nature in Asian Traditions of Thought*. Albany: State University of New York, 1989.

Clayton, Philip. *Mind and Emergence: From Quantum to Consciousness*. Oxford: Oxford University Press, 2004.

———. "Theology and the Physical Sciences." In *The Modern Theologians*, ed. David F. Ford and Rachael Muers, 342–56. 3rd ed. Oxford: Blackwell Publishing, 2005.

Cobb, John B., Jr. *Beyond Dialogue: Toward the Mutual Transformation of Christianity and Buddhism*. Philadelphia: Fortress Press, 1982.

———. *Christ in a Pluralistic Age*. Philadelphia: Westminster Press, 1975.

Cobb, John B., Jr., and Griffin, David Ray. *Process Theology: An Introductory Exposition*. Philadelphia: Westminster Press, 1976.

Cunningham, Lawrence H. *Thomas Merton and the Monastic Vision*. Grand Rapids, MI: William B. Eerdmans Publishing Company, 1999.

d'Aquili, Eugene, and Newberg, Andrew B. *The Mystical Mind: Probing the Biology of Religious Experience*. Minneapolis: Fortress Press, 1999.

Dawkins, Richard. *The Blind Watchmaker*. New York: W. W. Norton, 1986.

———. *River out of Eden*. New York: Harper Collins, 1995.

Dowe, Phil. *Galileo, Darwin, and Hawking: The Interplay of Science, Reason, and Religion*. Grand Rapids, MI: William B. Eerdmans Publishing Company, 2005.

Du Pre, George. "The Buddhist Philosophy of Science." In *Buddhism and Science*, ed. B. P. Kirtisinghe. Delhi: Motilal Press, 1984.

Dyson, Freeman. *Disturbing the Universe*. New York: Harper and Row, 1979.

Edelman, Gerald M. *Neural Darwinism: The History of Neuronal Group Selection*. New York: Basic Books, 1987.

Gilkey, Langdon. *Creationism on Trial*. Minneapolis: Winston Press, 1985.

———. *Maker of Heaven and Earth: The Christian Doctrine of Creation in Light of Modern Knowledge*. Garden City, NY: Doubleday, 1959.

———. *Nature, Science, and Religion: The Nexus of Science and Religion*. Minneapolis: Fortress Press, 1993.

————. *Religion and the Scientific Future*. New York: Harper and Row, 1970.

Gilson, Etienne. *The Christian Philosophy of Saint Augustine*. New York: Random House, 1960.

Gould, Stephen Jay. *Rocks of Ages: Science and Religion in the Fullness of Life*. New York: Ballantine Books, 1999.

Green, Brian. *The Elegant Universe*. New York: Vintage Books, 2003.

Guenther, H. V. *Matrix of Mystery: Scientific and Humanistic Aspects of rDzogs-chen Thought*. Boston: Shambala, 1984.

Guth, Alan, and Steinhard, Paul. "The Inflationary Universe." *Scientific American* 250 (May 1984): 116–28.

Habito, Ruben L. F. "The Resurrection of the Dead and Life Everlasting: From a Futuristic to a Realized Christianity," in *The Sound of Liberating Truth: Buddhist-Christian Dialogue in Honor of Frederick J. Streng*, ed. Sallie B. King and Paul O. Ingram. Surrey: Curzon Press, 1999.

————. *Zen Breath, Healing Breath: Zen Spirituality for a Wounded Earth*. Maryknoll, NY: Orbis Books, 1993.

Halliwell, Jonathan J. "Quantum Cosmology and the Creation of the Universe." In *Cosmology: Historical, Literary, Philosophical, Religious, and Scientific Perspectives*. New York: Garland Publishing, 1993.

Haught, John F. *Deeper Than Darwin: The Prospect Religion in an Age of Evolution*. Cambridge: Westview Press, 2003.

————. *God after Darwin: A Theology of Evolution*. Boulder, CO: Westview Press, 2000.

Hawking, Stephen W. *A Brief History of Time*. New York: Bantam, 1988.

Hefner, Philip. "Editorial." *Zygon* 35 (2000): 467–68.

Hesse, Mary, and Arbib, Michael. *The Construction of Reality*. New York: Cambridge University Press, 1986.

————. *A Briefer History of Time*. New York: Bantam Dell. 2005.

Hick, John. *An Interpretation of Religion*. New Haven, CT: Yale University Press, 1989.

Impey, Chris, and Petrey, Catherine. *Science and Theology: Ruminations on the Cosmos*. Rome: The Vatican Observation and the Templeton Foundation, 2002.

Ingram, Paul O. "Interfaith Dialogue as a Source of Buddhist-Christian Creative Transformation." In *Buddhist-Christian Dialogue: Mutual Renewal and Transformation*, ed. Paul O. Ingram and Frederick J. Streng, 77–94. Honolulu: University of Hawaii Press, 1986.

————. "A Reflection on Buddhist-Christian Dialogue with the Natural Sciences." In *Fifty Years in Science and Religion*, ed. Robert John Russell, 315–28. Burlington, VT: Ashgate Publishing, 2004.

————. "'That We May Know Each Other': The Pluralist Hypothesis as a Research Program." *Buddhist-Christian Studies* 24 (2004): 135–57.

James, William. *The Variety of Religious Experience*. New York: Longmans, Green, and Company, 1912.

Jammer, Max. *Einstein and Religion*. Princeton, NJ: Princeton University Press, 1999.

Jeannerod, Marc. "Are There Limits to the Naturalization of Mental States?" In *Neuroscience and the Person: Scientific Perspectives on Divine Action*, ed. Robert John

Russell, Nancy Murphy, Theo C. Meyering, and Michael A. Arbib, 119–28. Vatican City: Vatican Observatory Publications, 1999.

Johnston, Philip. *Silent Music: The Science of Meditation*. New York: Harper and Row, 1974.

Jordan, Robert. "Time and Contingency in St. Augustine." In *Augustine: A Collection of Critical Essays*, ed. R. A. Markus, 255–79. New York: Anchor Books, 1972.

Kato, Bunno, trans. *Myho-Renge-Kyo: The Sutra of the Lotus Flower of the Wonderful Law*. Tokyo: Kosei Publishing Company, 1971.

Katz, Steven T. "Language, Epistemology, and Mysticism." In *Mysticism and Philosophical Analysis*, ed. Steven T. Katz, 22–74. New York: Oxford University Press, 1978.

Keating, Thomas. *Invitation to Love: The Way of Christian Contemplation*. New York: Continuum Publications, 1997.

———. *Open Mind, Open Heart: The Contemplative Dimension of the Gospel*. New York: Continuum Publications, 1997.

Keenan, John P. "Some Questions about the World." In *The Sound of Liberating Truth: Buddhist-Christian Dialogues in Honor of Frederick J. Streng*, ed. Sallie B. King and Paul O. Ingram, 181–85. Surrey: Curzon Press, 1999.

———. "The Mind of Wisdom and Justice in the Letter of James." In *The Sound of Liberating Truth: Buddhist-Christian Dialogues in Honor of Frederick J. Streng*, ed. Sallie B. King and Paul O. Ingram, 186–99. Surrey: Curzon Press, 1999.

Knitter, Paul F. "Towards a Liberation Theology of Religions." In *The Myth of Christian Uniqueness: Toward a Pluralistic Theology of Religions*, ed. John Hick. Maryknoll, NY: Orbis Books, 1985.

Kraft, Kenneth. *Inner Peace, World Peace: Essays on Buddhism and Nonviolence*. Albany: State University of New York Press, 1992.

LeDoux, Joseph E. "Emotions: A View through the Brain." In *Neuroscience and the Person: Scientific Perspectives on Divine Action*, ed. Robert John Russell, Nancy Murphy, Theo C. Meyering, and Michael A. Arbib, 101–17. Vatican City: Vatican Observatory Publications, 1999.

MacKay, Donald M. *Brains, Machines, and Persons*. Grand Rapids, MI: William B. Eerdmans Publishing, 1980.

Mansfield, Victor. "Time in Madhyamika Buddhism and Modern Physics." *The Pacific World* 11–12 (1995–1996): 28–67.

Matteo, Anthony. "The Light of Reason: Evolutionary Psychology and Ethics." *Science and Spirit Magazine* (July–August 1999): 14–15, 42.

McFague, Sallie. *Metaphorical Theology: Models of God in Religious Language*. Philadelphia: Fortress Press, 1982.

———. *Models of God: Theology for an Ecological, Nuclear Age*. Minneapolis: Fortress Press, 1987.

Merton, Thomas. *The Asian Journal of Thomas Merton*. New York: New Directions Publishing Corporation, 1973.

———. *Mystics and Zen Masters*. New York: Dell Publishing, 1967.

———. "Monastic Experience and East-West Dialogue." In *The Asian Journal of Thomas Merton*, ed. Naomi Burton, et al., 309–25. New York: New Directions Books, 1973.

Midgley, Mary. *Science and Poetry*. London: Routledge, 2001.

———. *Science as Salvation*: London: Routledge, 1992.

Miller, Kenneth R. *Finding Darwin's God*. New York: Cliff Street Books, 1999.

Monod, Jacques. *Chance and Necessity*. New York: Vintage Books, 1972.

Murphy, Nancy. *Theology in the Age of Scientific Reasoning*. Ithaca, NY: Cornell University Press, 1990.

Murphy, Nancy, and Ellis, George F. R. *On the Moral Nature of the Universe: Theology, Cosmology, and Ethics*. Minneapolis: Fortress Press, 1996.

Nelson, Gene. "Carving a Discourse." *Science and Spirit* (January–February 2006): 15–17.

Newberg, Andrew B., d'Aquili, Eugene, and Rause, Vince, eds. *Why God Won't Go Away: Brain Science and the Biology of Belief*. New York: Ballantine, 2001.

Olcott, Henry Steel. *A Buddhist Catechism According to the Singhalese Canon*. London: Allen, Scott, 1889.

Pannenberg, Wolfhart. *Theology and the Philosophy of Science*. Philadelphia: Westminster Press, 1976.

Peacocke, Arthur. *Evolution: The Disguised Friend of Faith?* Philadelphia: Templeton Foundation Press, 2004.

———. *Theology for a Scientific Age: Being and Becoming—Natural, Divine, and Human*. Minneapolis: Fortress Press, 1993.

Persinger, Michael A. *Neuropsychological Bases of God Beliefs*. New York: Praeger, 1987.

Peters, Ted. *Science, Theology, and Ethics*. Burlington, VT: Ashgate Publishing, 2003.

Peters, Ted, Russell, Robert John, and Welker, Michael, eds. *Resurrection: Theological and Scientific Assessments*. Grand Rapids, MI: William B. Eerdmans Publishing Company, 2002.

Peterson, Gregory. *Minding God: Theology and the Cognitive Sciences*. Minneapolis: Fortress Press, 2003.

Polkinghorne, John. *Belief in God in an Age of Science*. New Haven, CT: Yale University Press, 1998.

———. *Reason and Reality*. Valley Forge, PA: Trinity Press International, 1991.

———. *The Faith of a Physicist*. Minneapolis: Fortress Press, 1996.

———. "The Metaphysics of Divine Action." In *Chaos and Complexity: Scientific Perspectives on Divine Action*, ed. Robert John Russell, Nancy Murphy, and Arthur R. Peacocke, 147–56. Vatican City: Vatican Observatory Publications, 2000.

———. *Quarks, Chaos, and Christianity*. New York: Crossroad, 1998.

Queen, Christopher S., ed. *Engaged Buddhism in the West*. Boston: Wisdom Publications, 2000.

———. "Introduction." In *Engaged Buddhism: Buddhist Liberation Movements in Asia*, ed. Christopher S. Queen and Sallie B. King, 1–44. Albany: State University of New York Press, 1996.

Redmond, Geoffrey P. "Comparing Science and Buddhism," *The Pacific World* 11–12 (1995–1996): 68–117.

Russell, Robert John. "Finite Creation without a Beginning: The Doctrine of Creation in Relation to Big Bang and Quantum Cosmologies." In *Quantum Cosmology and the Laws of Nature: Scientific Perspectives on Divine Action*, ed. Robert John Russell, Nancy Murphy, and C. J. Isham, 291–326. Vatican City: Vatican Observatory Publications, 1993.

——. "Intelligent Design Is No Science and Does Not Qualify Be Taught in Public School Science Classes." *Theology and Science* (July 2005): 131–32.

——. "Life in the Universe: Philosophical and Theological Issues." *CTNS Bulletin* 21, no. 2 (spring 2001): 3–9.

——. "Quantum Physics in Theological and Philosophical Perspective." In *Physics, Philosophy, and Theology: A Common Quest for Understanding*, ed. Robert John Russell, Willian R. Stoeger, and George V. Coyne, 343–74. Notre Dame: University of Notre Dame Press, 1988.

Russell, Robert John, Stoeger, William R., and Ayala, Francisco J., eds. *Evolutionary and Molecular Biology: Scientific Perspectives on Divine Action.* Vatican City: Vatican Observatory Foundation, 1998.

Sagan, Carl. *Cosmos.* New York: Random House: 1980.

Sanders, Nicholas. "Once More into the Breach: Divine Action and Modern Science." *Science and Spirit Magazine* (July–August 1999): 36–37.

Sells, Michael A. *Mystical Languages of Unsaying.* Chicago: University of Chicago Press, 1994.

Smith, Wilfred Cantwell. *Belief in History.* Princeton, NJ: Princeton University Press, 1979.

——. *Understanding Religious Life.* Belmont, CA: Wadsworth Publishing Company, 1985.

Stein, Ross L. "The Action of God in the World—A Synthesis of Process Thought in Science and Theology." *Theology and Science* 4 (2006): 64–65.

Stenmark, Mikael. *How to Relate Science and Religion.* Grand Rapids, MI: William B. Eerdmans Publishing Company, 2004.

Streng, Frederick J. *Emptiness: A Study in Religious Meaning.* Nashville: Abingdon Press, 1967.

Stoeger, William R. "Reflections on the Interaction of My Knowledge of Cosmology and My Christian Belief." *CTNS Bulletin* 21, no. 2 (spring 2001): 10–18.

Taniguchi, Shoyo. "Modern Science and Early Buddhist Ethics: Methodology of Two Disciplines." *The Pacific World* 11–12 (1995–1996): 45–53.

Teilhard de Chardin, Pierre. *The Future of Man.* New York: Harper and Row, 1959.

——. *The Phenomenon of Man.* New York: Harper & Row, 1959.

Tillich, Paul. *Systematic Theology I.* Chicago: University of Chicago Press, 1951.

Tipler, Frank. *The Physics of Immortality.* New York: Doubleday, 1994.

——. "The Omega Point as *Eschaton*: Answers to Pannenberg's Questions for Scientists." *Zygon* 24, no. 2 (June 1989): 217–53.

———. "The Omega Point Theory: A Model for an Evolving God." In *Physics, Philosophy, and Theology*, ed. Robert John Russell. Vatican City: Vatican Observatory, 1988.

Toolan, David S. "Praying in a Post-Einsteinian Universe." *Cross Currents* (winter 1996–1997): 437–70.

Torrance, Thomas. "God and the Contingent World." *Zygon* 14 (1979): 347.

Townes, Charles. "Marriage of Two Minds." *Science and Spirit* (January–February 2006): 36–43.

Tucker, Mary Evelyn, and Williams, Duncan Ryukan, eds. *Buddhism and Ecology*. Cambridge, MA: Harvard University, 1997.

Tweed, Thomas. *The American Encounter with Buddhism, 1844–1912*. Bloomington: Indiana University Press, 1992.

Van Hyussteen, J. Wentzel. *The Shaping of Rationality: Towards Interdisciplinarity in Theology and Science*. Grand Rapids, MI: William B. Eerdmans Publishing, 1999.

Wallace, B. Alan, ed. *Buddhism and Science: Breaking New Ground*. New York: Columbia University Press, 2003.

———. *Choosing Reality: A Buddhist View of Physics and the Mind*. Ithaca, NY: Snow Lion Publications, 1996.

Weinberg, Steven. *The First Three Minutes*. New York: Basic Books, 1988.

Wheeler, John Archibald. *At Home in the Universe*. New York: AIP Press, 1996.

Whitehead, Alfred North. *Process and Reality: Corrected Edition*, ed. David Ray Griffin and Donald W. Sherburne. New York: The Free Press, 1978.

Whitehouse, W. A. *Christian Faith and the Scientific Attitude*. New York: Philosophical Library, 1952.

Williams, George C. *The Pony Fish's Glow*. New York: Harper Collins, 1997.

Wilson, E. O. *On Human Nature*. Cambridge, MA: Harvard University Press, 1978.

Worthing, Mark William. *God, Creation, and Contemporary Physics*. Minneapolis: Fortress Press, 1996.

Index

About the Author

Paul O. Ingram received his Ph.D. in history of religions from the Clare-mont Graduate University. He was a member of the faculty in religious stud-ies at Simpson College, Indianola, Iowa, for nine years and the Department of Religion at Pacific Lutheran University, Tacoma, Washington, for thirty years. His most recent books include *The Sound of Liberating Truth: Buddhist-Christian Dialogue in Honor of Frederick J. Streng* (edited with Sallie B. King), *Wrestling with the Ox: A Theology of Religious Experience, Wrestling with God*, and an edited collection of essays entitled *Constructing a Relational Cosmol-ogy*. He served as vice president and president of the Society for Buddhist-Christian Studies and is a member of the Center for Process Studies (Clare-mont, California) and the Center for Theology and the Natural Sciences (Berkeley, California). After his retirement from Pacific Lutheran University in 2006, he relocated with his wife Regina to Mukilteo, Washington, where he now lives in deliberate simplicity.